WHEN
NATURE
SPEAKS —

THE LIFE OF
FORREST C. SHAKLEE, SR.

DEDICATION

When asked if there were a single heritage he would bequeath to the thousands of people who, like himself, responded to the voice of Nature, Dr. Shaklee replied without hesitation, "MY LIFE." It is therefore, to those people in the field that this chronicle of his life is gratefully dedicated.

WHEN
NATURE
SPEAKS —

THE LIFE OF
FORREST C. SHAKLEE, SR.

By Georges Spunt

ILLUSTRATED

Fell's Books Fill Your Needs

Frederick Fell Publishers, Inc.

NEW YORK, NEW YORK

LIBRARY OF CONGRESS CATALOGING IN PUBLICATION DATA

Spunt, Georges.
    When Nature Speaks.

    1. Shaklee, Forrest Clell. 2. Chiropractors--
California--Biography. 3. Shaklee Corporation--
History. I. Title.

RZ232.S5S68 1977   615'.534'0924 [B]   77-9916

ISBN: 0-8119-0279-X

For information address:

Frederick Fell Publishers, Inc.
386 Park Avenue South
New York, New York 10016

Published simultaneously in Canada by:
Thomas Nelson & Sons, Limited
Don Mills, Ontario, Canada

1 2 3 4 5 6 7 8 9 0

MANUFACTURED IN THE UNITED STATES OF AMERICA

Permissions

Mary D. Simonson, Jessie D. Lyon and Blanche D. Chase.

Acknowledgments

FIRST AND foremost we must thank Dr. Forrest C. Shaklee, Sr. for approving a definitive biography. And, having agreed to this record of his life, we are indebted to him for the hours spent together, scanning the past and gleaning the gems of that life, in what must have seemed to him an endless interrogation.

To Dorothy Shaklee we owe many thanks, for filling in facts that the overly modest subject of this book considered trifling. The repeated injunction, "Don't glorify me," echoes in our ears. And, we must thank Dorothy, as well, for searching among their possessions for clippings and photographs that would have been otherwise unavailable.

We owe both Forrest, Jr. and Raleigh Shaklee much appreciation for the perspectives that they were able to shed on their father, and for supplying the details of co-founding the enterprise that was to become The Shaklee Corporation. We are particularly grateful for the interview time granted at the cost of their busy schedules.

Thanks are in order to Alan Kennedy, Senior Vice-President Sales, and to J. Gary Shansby, President of Shaklee Corporation; the former for his original inspiration that the life of Forrest C. Shaklee, Sr. be written, and the latter for his prompt authorization of this biography.

Compiling the facts on a life as intricate and ever changing as that of Forrest C. Shaklee, Sr., required digging not only into immediate family and company archives, but necessitated as well, research in the areas where he grew up, was educated and trained, and where he practiced. In addition to hiring a professional researcher, we made a special journey to the land of Forrest Shaklee's birth, and contacted family and friends who knew him in his youth. For their cooperation in giving interviews and sharing documents and photographs, or for simply conducting tours of Dr. Shaklee's previous homes and office sites, we are indebted to the following family members: Edith Overton and her son Marvin, Gerald and Jean Smith, Christopher Columbus (Clarence) Epps, Jr., Ada Jo Howry, William Shaklee and Jacqueline Lyman.

Among Dr. Shaklee's colleagues, friends and acquaintances who provided insights on his life, we wish to thank Jack MacNider, Dr. Ralph Ulrich, Jack Dougherty, Truly Levorson, Rose Nehring, Floy Moretz Dahl, Mr. and Mrs. Dale Potter, Irma Harpole, Guy and Fern Fogler, Mr. and Mrs. Edgar Mahan, and Alena Scandrett.

For taking the time to answer questions, and for providing historical and geographical data, we wish to thank the following individuals, societies, universities and institutions: Maurine Coe of the Iowa State Historical Society; the Iowa State University; Palmer College of Chiropractic; Davenport Municipal Art Gallery; Wallace Homestead Co.; Mr. John Carter of the Nebraska State Historical Society; Mary Ruble of the Cocke County Historical Society, Tennessee; Robert Halgrim, Curator of Thomas Edison's Winter Home, Fort Myers, Florida; Mrs. Barbara Snedden, G.R.S., researcher.

And, finally, designating these acknowledgements under the editorial "we" is not incidental. For without the consistent efforts and sheer hard work of my assistant, Donna Pollard, this book could not have been written.

Foreword

CERTAIN ERAS of history are glorified, for example, the Golden Age of Greece, the Renaissance. Sometimes these epochs are narrowed to a decade, the Roaring Twenties or Gay Nineties. The turn of the century in Europe reflected a brilliance in the arts (Art Nouveau prevailed) and the gradual erosion of monarchies. For the United States it marked, almost imperceptibly, the emergence of the New World, through industry and manufacture.

To be sure, there was the glitter of New York Society's 400—the diamond horseshoe at the Metropolitan Opera House, Delmonico's Restaurant, where Diamond Jim Brady held court. It was a time of Lillian Russell, the Iowa born ideal of American beauty, and champagne drunk from silk slippers in the metropolises of New York, Chicago and San Francisco. But, in the heartland of America, the tone was industry, inventiveness, and the virtue of work was its own reward.

In 1890, Idaho and Wyoming became states under the presidency of Benjamin Harrison. "Gentlemen Jim" Corbett won the heavyweight boxing title by defeating John L. Sullivan. Walt Whitman, a poet who sang of America, died. Three years later, a successful soap merchant resigned from his position to become a writer; Elbert Hubbard created widespread interest in his "Little Journeys" series and achieved fame for his book, A MESSAGE TO GARCIA. William Jennings Bryan, who had successfully barnstormed the countryside with the Chautauqua lectures, was defeated for the presidency by William McKinley. The rail strike of 1894, brought to prominence a young attorney named Clarence Darrow, for his defense in the conspiracy charges brought against Eugene Debs. It was in the nineties too, that the first American comic strip, "Katzenjammer Kids" appeared, and America went to war with Spain defeating the Spanish fleet at Manila.

Shortly after Karl Benz had built his four-wheel car in Germany, Henry Ford developed and built his first automobile. Thomas Edison was working on improving a film projector by Thomas Armat, which he sold as the Edison Vitascope. George Washington Carver, after repeated attempts at enrolling in Southern universities, was admitted to Iowa State University. And, in the little town of Carlisle in Iowa, a child named Forrest Shaklee was born.

It might strike one as pretentious, perhaps even impertinent, to chronicle this birth with international events and titans of American business. The fact remains that Hubbard, Bryan, Darrow, Edison and others, impacted on a personal level, the life of Dr. Forrest Shaklee. What is his claim to fame? In terms of corporate success, the business he founded with his two sons, Forrest, Jr. and Raleigh (Lee) some twenty years ago, is flourishing. But, when measured against the bonanzas of great fortunes, his is minor.

What sets Forrest Shaklee apart is his rarified approach to life, and the philosophies which he applied to business. Before the imperilment of our environment became a world concern, long before the word "ecology" had gained currency, Forrest Shaklee had made his covenant with Nature. "Nature is our sole supplier," he says. "And when Nature speaks—we listen." If that were all, it might merely be accepted as the kind of serendipitous phenomenon, when the time of an idea and the idea itself collide fortuitously. Add to that a man who developed and used as the basis for his life's work, the credo of Thoughtsmanship. This is no idle slogan, but in fact, a paraphrasing of the Biblical, "Whatsoever he thinketh in his heart so is he," which in Forrest Shaklee's interpretation becomes, "What you think you look; what you think you do; what you think you are." Thoughtsmanship, a basic, simple and eminently workable philosophy, is the subject of a book by Dr. Shaklee titled, REFLECTIONS ON A PHILOSOPHY. In addition to the concerns of Nature and a guiding philosophy, Dr. Shaklee and his sons imbued their co-workers and field sales force with the principle of The Golden Rule. While, of course, such a principle cannot and should not be legislated, it has proven highly successful in the Company's relations with the independent sales force and vice versa. The very fact that the Golden Rule exists as a policy in the corporate world of the twentieth century, is in itself extraordinary.

Dr. Shaklee is a modest man. Compliment him on his achievements, and he will quickly inform you that, "This is not a one-man movement. Our business success has been due to the cooperative effort of the thousands of men and women who make up the whole Shaklee family."

Dismissing the past appears to be characteristic of dynamic men. In his autobiography, Clarence Darrow says, "For the most part, I seldom think about my ancestors; but I had them. . . .In fact, I could fill this book with their names if I knew them all and deemed it the least worth."[1]

In 1916 Henry Ford went on record as saying, "History is bunk! It is tradition. We want to live in the present and the only history that is worth a tinker's damn is the history we make today."[2]

Forrest Shaklee, Sr., when approached on the subject of his biography, expressed somewhat similar sentiments. Said Dr. Shaklee, paraphrasing Mark Twain, "I have never really cared to look up my family tree for fear I might see a horse-thief hanging from a limb." (Our research failed to uncover anything to substantiate such fears.)

Dr. Shaklee's reasons are based mainly on the fact that he is an inventive man with an eye to the future. Each yesterday for him tends to be a buried past. In fact, he frequently says "To heck with yesterday—what's doing today?"

Today is a significant word for Forrest Shaklee. Says he, "Today is the most important day of your life. But how are you living this life? *As a man thinketh in his heart so is he.* And so your life will be exactly what you *think* to make it."

Regardless, history is our only record. If for nothing other than the experience to be gained, it is worth the researching and the chronicling. When he livened to the project, Dr. Shaklee proved to be an incredible source of anecdotal treasures, many of which might not have come to light because of his indifference to history.

While history for its sentimental value may not have much meaning to Dr. Shaklee, he is fascinated by beginnings, and will quite readily relate the exact occurrence of some idea that grew to fruition. "In the beginning," is one of his favorite gambits—"if there *was* a beginning, and I suppose there had to be, (or I wouldn't be here) there was creative energy—life force." So, let us review the forces which contributed to the beginning of Forrest Clell Shaklee, Sr.

WHEN
NATURE
SPEAKS—

THE LIFE OF
FORREST C. SHAKLEE, SR.

Part I

IN THE BEGINNING

Chapter I

AMERICANS ARE, by nature, peripatetic. Whether the migratory trend began as need for space or fertile farm lands or, as in the case of the Mormons, for lands to worship as they chose, had best be left to a sociologist to define. But, we do not need a sociologist to analyze the great migratory sweep from East to West in the eighteen hundreds. The news of the discovery of gold at Sutter's Mill in California, caused an explosion of travel in 1849 which did not taper off until the late fifties. Thousands upon thousands made the long trek by crude ox-pulled farm wagons, or by Conestogas with horse teams. Many perished of disease or drowned in river crossings on rudely lashed-together barges. Whole families were decimated by either cholera, starvation, wagon-train bandits or Indian raids—and still the wagons rolled and thundered across the plains.

This widespread exodus caused its share of economic consternation. The newspapers of the times lamented of the high rates of labor caused by the depopulation of farmers and mechanics in such states as Ohio, Indiana and Illinois. The Cleveland *Plain Dealer,* deplored the situation—"What will be the end of these things? It is a grave question."

We can only guess at what caused the Southern aristocrat, George Washington Epps, to mount a wagon train and leave his home in Tennessee. As a young man, Epps had committed the unpardonable sin, in the eyes of the ante-bellum South, by his elopement with a servant girl. This union secured for Epps disinheritance and banishment from the family plantation in Virginia. The Epps plantation, some of which is still standing, is reputed to be the oldest land grant in United States history, dating back to 1632. It is further said that the plantation is where Abraham Lincoln stayed overnight before he signed the truce at Appomatox Court House.

In 1850, or thereabouts, Epps' wife died, leaving him thirteen children. His father died a short while earlier, and Epps petitioned the estate for a share of the inheritance. Since he was, in due course, granted a sum of money, we can assume it was on the proviso that he leave the South. Though by now a man in his late fifties, Epps was eager to start anew. Whether or not he had heard the cry of "Gold!" and was headed for California, we cannot be sure, but, since he eventually settled with his family in Iowa, we are inclined to believe that the major impetus was a life free of the South's social mores and their attendant restrictions. Not all of his children were quite that willing to sever their ties with the South. We know that while John Winston, Peter Frances and William George Sylvester, accompanied their father and the brood of younger children, another son, James Edwin, elected to remain behind with his wife, Anna Goldsbury. The Goldsburys, including another daughter, Mary, also joined the Epps train.

A time in early spring, when the snow had melted on the high pastures, was the scheduled starting day for wagons westward. And, if the train was to leave in the latter part of April, months of preparation were needed. Certainly Epps would have begun by following the already established tradition of Wagon Train organization. This was to elect officers and a council of elders to make and uphold by-laws for the journey. Wagons were grouped in divisions of two, each consisting of equal platoons of wagons and each division headed by an officer. While the guidebooks could lead one to river crossings and pastures, a pilot who had previously made the journey and who was familiar with the terrain had to be hired. A scout who could act as rifleman against hostile Indians or marauding wagon bandits was necessary, too.

Given the character of George Washington Epps, we might safely assume that his own wagons were the heavy and costly Conestogas, and that they were horse or mule-drawn.

[1]The Conestoga wagon was first built in the mid-eighteenth century by Germans in the Conestoga Valley. They were used primarily for hauling produce to Philadelphia and Baltimore, and were actually descendants from the low-wheeled freight and passenger stage wagons of Europe. Quite often, in the tradition of the Pennsylvania Dutch, the wagons were brightly painted in blues and brilliant scarlet; some of the fancier ones had designs stencilled on the body. Tow canvas was woven to be stretched over hoops to cover passengers and freight. The horses were bred heavy and were nearly always black. Their bridles were decorated with scarlet tassels and above each pair of hames, a chime of bells was mounted. The courtly Epps would have seen to it as well, that the construction of his wagon was equal to the standards (or lack of them) of the roads. The wagon would have to be built with high wheels affording the axletrees room to clear stumps and boulders.

The matter of provisions must be considered. While we do not have a record of the Epps' train provisions, we can estimate roughly by comparable wagon trains what items were required. For wagons drawn by four-to-six-horse teams, a major item would be horse feed. There would, of course, be some kegs of water, sacks of flour, cornmeal, buckwheat, dried beans and rice, tins of sea-biscuit and crackers. Other than what could be hunted enroute, the meat supply would consist of dried beef, legs of smoked ham and flitches of bacon. Fruits were dry; raisins, apples, peaches. Staples included coffee and tea, crushed sugar, molasses, kegs of pickles, preserves and vinegar, and at least one keg of brandy, ostensibly for medicinal purposes.[2]

In the Epps household, the women would surely have packed silk hoods, sunbonnets, merino wool dresses, and soft leather gloves. Down pillows, sheets, blankets and table-cloths would not be forgotten. For rougher wear, the women would bring linsey dresses and calico wrappers, poke bonnets, shoes as well as boots for wading, and the necessary accoutrements for mending and darning. Men and boys brought cloaks, suits, India rubber topcoats, hats, shoes, boots. Boys wore sturdy jeans, box jackets, caps and boots. An abundance of socks was advised. Wooden chests, hair trunks and carpet bags were used to store clothing and valu-ables.[3]

Arms, and hunting weapons as well, were part of the equipment. Flintlocks, powder and lead, with a mold to cast bullets were required, as well as butcher knives, axes, and rope to stake the horses while they grazed. Heavier equip-ment, such as a farmer might use, were taken with discre-tion since the wagons could not be overloaded.[4]

The road to Oregon and California, called the National Road, began in Baltimore, crossed Pennsylvania, and by 1833, was extended to Columbus, Ohio. In 1852, an unpaved trail was added from Indiana to Vandalia, Illinois.[5]

We do not know to what extent the Epps train followed the National Road, but we do know that George Washington Epps went from Tennessee to Kentucky, probably catching the National Road in Indiana, where he left the wagon train to proceed to Putman County and the town of Green Castle. Whether or not he had had a previous encounter with an eighteen-year-old girl named Mary Jane Bagley, we are uncertain, but the effect of this young lady was enough to cause George to remain in Green Castle. Headed by William George Sylvester, acting as *chef de famille,* the wagons continued on the unpaved section of the National Road from Indiana to Illinois.

Joining the train at this juncture, were the Shaklee and Overton families, who had made the trek independently from

Ohio. Reverend David Shaklee, a man of about thirty, was a follower of Alexander Campbell and a minister of the Christian Church. David, garbed in clerical black, was a tall man, with an austere demeanor. Under the preacher's hat, his hair fell to the shoulders. A beard flowed almost to his waist. His voice was resonant and impelling. With David was his wife Rachel, their young daughters, Margaret, Rebecca and Sarah. The Shaklee ancestry was from Ireland, probably County Kildare. A branch of the family had migrated in 1774 and had fought with some distinction in the Revolution. The descendants, who went by several appellations, include Shakle, Shekel, Schacklee, Schackley, and Shaklee, became for the most part farmers and were devoutly religious.

The Overtons had come to the States earlier from Holland. Eli Overton, Sr., born in 1692, had emigrated to New York as a young man and had helped sponsor the Revolutionary War, by furnishing arms and gunpowder. His son, Eli Overton, Jr., had served with the Revolutionary forces. With the typical proliferation of a name, common to the nineteenth century, Eli, Jr. called *his* son Eli, and he was eventually known as Old Eli. Old Eli and his children, among whom was a son named David, were part of the train headed West. David, born in 1836, was a robust, stocky lad and so expert a marksman, that he had been elected scout and rifleman for the expedition. He had formed an attachment to the Shaklee family and the minister regarded him as a younger brother.

The initial encounter between the Epps wagons and the Shaklee-Overton contingent, must have been dramatic. The Southerners, albeit somewhat down at the heel, had managed with their colorful wagons, division officers wearing cloaks, their women in silk hoods and carrying parasols, a certain inimitable flair. In contrast, the immigrants from Ohio had traveled in prairie schooners. These were essentially rough farm wagons with sturdy wheels. The body of the wagon was flat and solidly bolted to its undercarriage. Duck canvas lashed over curved bows formed the cover. Barrels, chests, and some farming implements were secured by rope to the sides or front of the body.[6]

They had used oxen to pull their wagons. Oxen were somewhat cheaper than mules or horses and generally conceded to be stronger. There were some disadvantages to oxen since they were slower than horses and mules and who, because they can't sweat, need time to pause and cool off. What cows David Shaklee brought, he wisely kept unyoked, having learned from the accounts of other immigrants that cows forced to pull wagons a great distance fared badly. What milk they produced was unfit to drink, and the mortality rate among yoked cows was extremely high.[7]

Over his black ministerial garb, David Shaklee wore a long black oilcloth coat to protect him from the elements. The women wore calico, sunbonnets, and made do with sacks in place of shawls. Boys dressed in hickory shirts, rough shirts, rough pants and wore kip boots, made of the undressed hides of small animals. Provisions were basic, and besides the usual staples, they had brought green walnuts, hazel nuts, raw sugar, cheese, soap, sperm candles, blankets, coarse towels and such camp essentials as water buckets, camp kettles, rough nails, ropes, pegs and tents.[8]

The Epps children, motherless and now at least temporarily fatherless, touched the heart of Rachel Shaklee, and she drew them to her.

As for William George Sylvester, after dealing with the wheelwrights for the repair of wagons, and farriers to shoe his horses, blacksmiths to mend yokes and chains, he was very glad to have the skilled and practical David Shaklee assume leadership. Meanwhile, young David Overton, the scout-rifleman, had taken a fancy to William's sister-in-law, the pretty Mary Goldsbury.

Undoubtedly, the group from Ohio had traveled the National Road, but how far West they were heading is questionable. The promised land of Oregon and the gold of California are not likely to have been their objectives.

The revolution that had been fought to guarantee,

among other liberties, the right to religious freedom was not yet fifty years old when the country was swept by religious intolerance. The Mormons suffered cruelly in Illinois where their prophet Joseph Smith II was murdered, largely because of their anti-slavery beliefs. They were driven out of Missouri and, beginning in 1846, found a temporary haven in Iowa.[9]

In the mid-nineteenth century, the Christian Church proffered new concepts and its founder, Alexander Campbell, moved from Pennsylvania to Ohio and Virginia. With a tolerance that was to become characteristic of Iowans, both national and religious immigrants were treated with respect and aided in their pursuits.

We have no account of the journey from Illinois to Iowa, but it was there that the wagon train finally stopped. The artist Edwin Blashfield has memorialized wagon train settlers in a mural in the State House at Des Moines. This mural at the top of the Capitol stairs, depicts an ox-drawn prairie schooner driven by an ethereal woman in flowing white garb, who appears to be paying no attention to where they are going. Overhead, angels are seen swooping, presumably guiding the wagon in the right direction, while the men are walking along beside it.

In view of the privation and hardship of the journey which he experienced, David Shaklee would most likely have agreed with the early settler, who upon seeing this idealized concept said, "There was no durned angels when I come."[10]

Chapter II

WHEN THE Shaklee, Overton and Epps wagon trains converged on Iowa, it had been a state less than ten years. Before describing life at that time, we need to delve further into history and review the development of this bountiful state.

In his book, IOWA INSIDE OUT,[1] Herb Hake tells us that Iowa was, of course, first settled by Indians. The earliest pottery-bearing sites date roughly from 1000 B.C. These Indians were called Woodland Indians, because they were, in a sense, Iowa's first farmers. And, they were so named to distinguish them from the Archaic (non-farming) Indians who were nomadic hunters of an earlier time. The Woodland Indians built burial mounds, much like those that are seen in the countryside of China. Religious cults influenced the shapes of these mounds; some were conical, others linear, and some were built in effigies of birds and animals and were reserved for Indians of high rank.

Although the mounds in Northeast Iowa remain as a National Monument, the fate of these industrious and energetic Woodland Indians is uncertain. Around 1200 A.D., a warlike group of Indians from upper Mississippi arrived in Iowa. One of these Mississippi tribes were the Oneota, who were cannibals. It is speculated that the Oneota may have simply devoured the Mound Builders.

With the arrival of the French in the sixteenth century, the Oneota moved out of Eastern Iowa occupying the areas of the other tribes which began an exodus from East to West.

While France, in the persons of Father Marquette and Louis Joliet, must be given credit for first recognizing the importance of the Mississippi Valley, Spain laid claim to it some time before. Since Columbus and 1492, Spain's main quest had been for gold. They had not found it in the new

26

continent and didn't bother with settling the area. There was a tacit agreement between European nations that the discovery of a country gave the discovering nation title to the soil, but that the title must be consummated by possession. So, if the French knew about the Spanish claim, it didn't stop them from making their discoveries, and the King of England had John Cabot make a foray in 1497, claiming the whole continent for England.

Only the Indians didn't make claims. And, it never occurred to them that others had. They reasoned that since land belonged to the Great Spirit, it could not be owned by human beings. They were in for a rude awakening.

With Julien Dubuque, the period of French exploitation of the Indians began. Dubuque, a fur trader and the first settler in Iowa, used a rather nasty ruse to persuade the Fox Indians to let him operate their lead mines. Herb Hake relates that Kettle Chief, head of the tribe, staunchly resisted all Dubuque's blandishments, countering with a simple, "Ugh, Ugh," which meant then what it means now.

Dubuque persisted, arguing more persuasively.

"Ugh, Ugh," maintained Kettle Chief.

Then Dubuque had an accomplice pour oil upstream on Catfish Creek which ran by the Chief's encampment.

Once more Dubuque petitioned for the mines, and in so doing cast a burning brand from the campfire on the water which immediately burst into flames. Kettle Chief saw the light. "Ugh, *huh*," he said, which also meant then what it means now.

For some time, Dubuque did a thriving business in lead bars and fur pelts, which he shipped to St. Louis. But, business affairs were not the Frenchman's forte, and he ended up in debt.[2]

Hake tells us there were a couple of other Frenchmen who, with the endorsement of the Spanish, settled in Iowa. One of these planted the first, albeit unsuccessful, apple orchards.

But, harmony between the French and Indians did not

last too long. Trouble brewed between the traders and the Fox and Sauk tribes, whom the French had forced out of Michigan into Iowa. The war that broke out in 1754 was called the French and Indian War, but technically it was between the French and British. France lost the war and with it, Canada and part of Louisiana east of the Mississippi. This was, of course, before the Revolution and the founding of the United States.

France had been America's ally during the Revolution, but by 1800, she had undergone her own revolution. Napoleon Bonaparte was Emperor and he had wrested Western Louisiana from the Spanish. New Orleans represented a bottleneck in Mississippi traffic, and this gave the French control of that traffic, a thought that made President Jefferson very uneasy. Since Napoleon was in the thick of European wars and needed money, Jefferson hit upon the idea of buying New Orleans and West Florida from him. With $2,000,000 that Congress had been able to pungle up, James Monroe went to France to make that bid. Napoleon was not interested in piecemeal purchases and counter-offered to sell the whole of the Louisiana Territory for $15,000,000.

This was considerably more than Jefferson had either expected or was ready for, but he realized the enormous opportunity and seized it. The Louisiana Purchase was negotiated in 1803 with the final transfer of territory made in March of 1804, which is when Iowa first became part of the United States.

It was then America's turn to explore the area, which they did beginning with two expeditions—one up the Missouri with Lewis and Clark, the other up the Mississippi with Zebulon Pike. They liked what they saw, and it wasn't very long before the resident Indians realized that, while the Americans were not as coercive as either the Spanish, British or French, they had the same end in mind. The murder of a couple of settlers on Sauk territory brought about American demands for reparation. The Sauk and Fox tribes who didn't think two settlers on Indian soil amounted to very much, ignored American demands for a delegation of all the Sauk and Fox nations. They sent a few minor chiefs who, soon cozened by plenty of firewater, signed away their land east of the Mississippi, amounting to what is now Illinois and Wisconsin, to say nothing of a large area west of the Mississippi, and north of the Missouri river.[3]

Black Hawk, a Sauk warrior, was mightily incensed at this turn of events. And, when the Americans built a poorly situated fort on the Mississippi river at the head of the Des Moines rapids, Black Hawk badgered the fort with flaming arrows, sniping at and scalping any soldier unfortunate enough to venture outside the barracks. The war of 1812 between England and America gave Black Hawk his chance, and he and the Fox, Sauk and Ioway tribes joined the British against the Americans. By 1813 the fort named after President Madison was deemed indefensible, set afire, and abandoned. All that remains of the fort today is a brick chimney.[4]

Counting heavily on the support of friendly tribes and British aid, Black Hawk went on to harrass the Americans, until finally in 1832, there was an all-out war between them.

Black Hawk's forces of 400 Sauk warriors, their wives, and children were soon hounded by thousands of soldiers and, eventually, the 150 remaining men, women and children attempting to cross the Mississippi, were decimated. The war had lasted three months. Black Hawk was taken in chains to Washington, where Andrew Jackson, who was now President, wanted to see him. The sixty-five year old warrior held his chained hands in front of him and declared, "I am a man as you are." Jackson at once gave the order to free the Indian.[5]

Black Hawk was allowed to return to Iowa where he spent his remaining six years writing his life story. In it, he said, . . ."The white men do not scalp the head but they do worse, they poison the heart. It is not pure with them. . ." Upon his death he was given the full ceremonial burial place in a seated position in his grave. But, even there Black Hawk was to find no permanent peace. His grave was robbed and the exhumed corpse exhibited in a sideshow for a number of years. Finally, it was removed to a museum in Burlington, but it was as if the rage of Black Hawk could not be abated even in death. The museum burned to the ground and the bones of the mighty brave were reduced to ashes.[6]

Descendents of the settlers recognized the courage and honor of this Indian hero and to perpetuate his memory, called themselves Hawkeyes, which to this date remains a synonym for Iowans.[7]

After the Black Hawk War, as it was called, a treaty was drawn up between the Americans and the Sauk and Fox nations which ceded the eastern third of Iowa to the United States.

Keokuk, Chief of the Sauk tribes, who had attempted to disuade Black Hawk from resisting the Americans, was permitted to keep four hundred sections of land along the Iowa river. This last four years, and within nine, Keokuk and his people had been pushed as far west as Kansas.[8]

The exodus from Iowa of the Sauk, Fox, Pottawattamies and Winnebagos (who had also been transplanted to Iowa from Wisconsin and hated it) took nineteen years, and for every Indian removed from his land, there was an eager white settler ready to stake a claim on it. The Sioux hung on until 1851, when, upon selling their lands, they were moved to the Dakota Territory.[9]

It must be said that Americans never took lands without signing treaties and paying the Indians. The fact that when more Indian land was needed the treaties were abrogated, is another matter. The money paid was meager by American, but large by Indian standards. Much Indian land was acquired through their failure to meet credit obligations. Like most people new to a credit system, the Indians overbought and overcharged and were suddenly faced with having their loans called. While, undeniably, both the Europeans and Americans played on Indian needs for guns

30

and powder and their weakness for trinkets and whisky, perhaps the factor which contributed most to their debilitation, was internecine strife. There was constant warring among the Indian nations. And, this too, was played upon with unerring diplomatic skill by the white people.

From being part of the Louisiana territory, Iowa had become part of the Territory of Missouri in 1812, where it remained until Missouri became a state nine years later. There was some confusion over the dividing line which culminated in the Honey War. This opera bouffe situation occurred when the Missourians cut down some trees with prized beehives, in what the Iowans maintained was their territory. Troops on both sides were mobilized and feelings ran high, but not a shot was fired, and eventually the whole matter was dropped.[10]

In 1834 Iowa became part of the Michigan Territory and in 1836, it became part of Wisconsin Territory. This included all the future states of Wisconsin, Minnesota and parts of North and South Dakota.

There was, from the early settler days, a tough-minded independence about Iowans, so it was not surprising that they viewed becoming a state with very little enthusiasm.

In 1840, with over 40,000 settlers, less than 4,000 went to the polls and the majority voted against statehood. Two years later, with nearly double the population, the measure was again defeated.

Finally on December 28, 1846, Iowa entered the union as the 29th state, being paired with Florida, a slave state, to maintain the balance of power between the North and the South. At this time there were twenty-seven organized counties with a population of nearly 100,000 and settlements were pushing toward the Missouri river. By the time the Shaklee, Overton, Epps wagons rolled into Carlisle in the mid 1850's, Iowa's population exceeded 200,000.

Legend has it that Iowa got its name when an Indian crossed the Mississippi and, overcome by the fertile beauty of the land, called out, "Ayooez"—Indian for beautiful land.[11]

What one wonders, were the thoughts of the weary immigrants from Tennessee and Ohio when they sighted what was to be their future home?

Chapter III

PERHAPS WHAT gave David Shaklee an affinity for Carlisle was that it was named after a town in Pennsylvania. More likely, it was the untrammeled beauty of the place itself.

In 1843, a man named Jeremiah Church had entered a claim on land two miles northeast of Carlisle on the Des Moines river, which he named Dudley. In 1851, a great flood totally devastated the town. Among the flood legends was one that, "Uncle Jerry himself sat up high and dry in a tree and played his beloved fiddle during the flood." Undaunted, Church then secured the tract of land on which Carlisle now stands and, with the help of another man, laid out the new town.[1]

Carlisle is about twelve miles southeast of Des Moines, and is the same distance southward to Indianola, the county seat. East lies the fertile Des Moines river valley, while the northern boundary is close to the wooded banks of North River. From North River across the plain called Buffalo Prairie by these early settlers, to the Middle River on the south, is a level span, roughly two miles wide. The village was established among the rolling hills with a general store, a harness shop, a blacksmith shop, a wood lot and a flour mill which gave employment to many of the new settlers. David Shaklee homesteaded eighty acres of land. Since the land consisted of basins and hills, and since farmers do not live among their crops, David built a sturdy house of black walnut on the highest rise. He used his land for farming in summer, but, to provide for his family in winter, David went to work in the coal mines situated about three miles west of Carlisle.

Life in those early settler days is described by Mabel Owens Shaffer, in HISTORY OF CARLISLE AND VICINITY:[2]

33

. . ."Early Carlisle included a number of modest homes and a few more pretentious ones. The main street ran east and west on the hill above the business section, and a couple of blocks north, a district now occupied by homes and churches. This street is extra wide and attractive: it was called Market Street and was built wider to accomodate hitching racks to which were tied riding horses, teams and wagons, horses and buggies. Folks travelled more leisurely in those days but finally arrived at their destination and usually in one piece. The sights along the way were thoroughly observed by the travellers and a little trip was a favorite form of relaxation. . .The social life of Carlisle centered in schools and churches."

From the beginning, in Iowa it was said, "Build a church and raise a school." Like the rest of Iowa, Warren County responded with what amounted to fervor. Iowa's rate of literacy has, for many years. been the nation's highest. The first public school in Iowa was opened in 1830; the first in Carlisle was built in 1853. The schools served as the hub for merriment as well as learning, and school bands provided entertainment for the town folk. The bands vied with each other for colorful costumes and the mothers of the young musicians were kept busy fashioning them. The four early churches in Carlisle were: Baptist, Brethren, Methodist and Christian.

David Shaklee had much in common with the founders of the Christian church, Thomas and Alexander Campbell. Although the Campbells were originally Scottish, they had, like David's family, migrated from Ireland. And, like Alexander Campbell, David was a man of the earth and a persuasive orator. Alexander Campbell became pastor of the Brush Run Church in Pennsylvania. Later he had established Buffalo Seminary in Bethany, Virginia, specifically for the training of preachers. Since Margaret, David's oldest daughter, was born in Virginia, it is not inconceivable that David Shaklee had been ordained by Alexander himself. The principle difference between the Christian Church, or the Disciples of Christ, and the Baptists was the interpretation of baptism. Campbell published an enormously popular periodical, "The Christian Baptist," in which he excoriated missions, Sunday Schools and sectarian societies as then conducted. For this the Campbellites were ousted by the Baptist Association. Campbell, anticipating this action, had recruited his followers and organized a new church. Eventually, the Disciples of Christ became merged with another group, the Christian Connection, an amalgam of three groups, Methodists, Baptists and Presbyterians, and they were commonly known as the Christians. Believing that a better translation of the English Bible was needed and because of his mastery of it, Campbell did his own translation. His interest in the second coming of Christ caused him to suspend publication of the Christian Baptist, replacing it with the Millenial Harbinger.

It was, of course, with Campbell's version of the Bible and his tracts published in the Millenial Harbinger, that David Shaklee preached to his flock. Campbell roundly opposed the Baptist allocation of four circuits for one rural minister, but in those early settler days, in addition to officiating at the Christian Church in Carlisle, David made his circuit from town to town on horseback in fair or inclement weather. That his was a powerfully magnetic personality, is attested to by his grandson, Forrest Shaklee, who was only four when David died, just before the turn of the century. Forrest recalls the awesome and striking figure of his grandfather, erect on horseback, the hair now silver, cascading to his shoulders, the waist-length beard trimmed neatly, one hand aloft invoking the Almighty, the other swift and incisive to pound a point home on the Bible.

"The power of that voice was such," says Forrest, "that often when I have stood to address thousands of people, I have felt myself occupied by the presence of my grandfather, my gestures become his gestures, my voice, his. Peculiarly I feel as though my hair has lengthened and I almost stroke the beard, that I know consciously, I don't have. . ."

But, we are going ahead of ourselves. In the early fifties, the drawing power of the churches in the overall scheme of community life was such that it combined drama, entertainment and social life with religiosity and the comforting balm of salvation. Mabel Owen Shaffer relates that Sunday night services were the peak of social and religious activity of the week. One early settler told of the time when she and her fiance drove in from the country one Sunday evening, and went to each of the four Carlisle churches, but found no room in any of them. All were crowded to overflowing, with some people standing and others outside listening in at the windows.[3]

Along with David and Rachel Shaklee, the other wagon train families were also settling down. Old Eli Overton and his wife, Alsie, homesteaded land in nearby Polk County, and, with their sons Calvin, Ephraim, William and young David, began farming it.

The Epps family were in due time rejoined by the paterfamilias, George, who appeared with his new-found bride, Mary Jane Bagley. Life was primitive for these pioneers. Rachel Shaklee, Alsie Overton, and the young Mrs. Epps made all of their own, as well as their family's clothing. Neighboring women showed them how to weave their own cloth and they spun yarn to knit stockings and mittens. The men trapped small fur-bearing animals with which the woods abounded so that the pelts of fox, muskrat, beaver and racoons were fasioned into caps, collars and muffs.

Besides being the meeting place, where news and gossip were exchanged, the general store provided other necessities; muslin, calico and denim, sewing and household utensils and tools. There were, of course, the usual staples, and some simple remedies, including a cure for snakebite. A pioneer is on record, describing those early times: "There wasn't much style put on in those days. Comfort took its place. There were no fancy fixings like bouillon, salads and ices. A few slices of steak from a saddle of venison fried in the fireplace, some molasses from the jug under the kitchen table, some corn coffee piping hot, sufficed our needs. With such a meal we soon forgot the day's hard work."[4]

In those pre-railroad days when drayage was by wagons, the costs of even the most necessary staples were astronomical, and this settler tells of salt costing nine dollars a barrel, flour at ten dollars a sack—"and not guaranteed at that," and of paying a dollar for eight pounds of sugar. As for competitive pricing, there was none, the general store was *it*. Lamenting further on the high costs of food stuffs, he bemoans the price of coffee: "Even green coffee cost thirty cents a pound. This we took home and roasted before grinding. We were glad enough to get it green."[5]

Many of the settlers could scarcely afford even thirty cents for the luxury of coffee; a handy and common substitute was roasted and ground corn or barley. Forrest Shaklee recalls that barley, roasted and ground, was the coffee substitute used in their home, when they could not afford coffee beans.

Convenience and service was unknown in the context of shopping: "When the molasses jug was empty we took it to the store ourselves to get it filled. We usually had a piece of stout cord, or rope run through the handle of the jug, and thus we carried it suspended from the shoulder; sometimes we poked a stick through the handle and carried it over our shoulder. . ."

Bartering became a common practice and continued for many years, and Rachel would trade flats of fresh laid eggs for flour or yarn or cloth. Others would bring in daily churned butter. Likewise, the men proved their versatility—a carpenter could be expected to make cabinets and furniture. He might build looms, spinning wheels, wagons and even houses. Because coffin making insured a steady income, it was a frequent adjunct to these skills.

In an early account of Iowa, we learn of one man who

came there in 1855 and who, in addition to these accomplishments, "was also a blacksmith, made tools, sharpened plows and shod horses and oxen; and as a cooper he made tubs and barrels in his shop. From his casket making, he turned his hand to becoming the local undertaker. He did some dentistry and doctored his neighbors with simple remedies when they were ill. He had been a Methodist preacher from the age of twenty-one and attended to the spiritual wants of the people as well as their physical necessities. . ."[6]

So, it was natural, in that ambience, for David Shaklee to farm his land, bring his grist of wheat in sacks to the Carlisle Flour Mill for grinding, chop his timber and work in the coal mines. Besides his regular schedules of preaching, David's spiritual services included the christening of babies and, when they became youths, counseling them in their life's patterns. He officiated at their weddings and gave sermons at their funerals. He was sought to provide solace for the mourners.

It was a muscular existence for all the pioneers. Community spirit was high and the mood cooperative. Calvin Overton is recorded as having assisted in digging what is known even today as the "Cutoff," where the Des Moines river was cut through below the site of where Dudley had been, shortening the channel by three miles.

John Winston Epps became engrossed in the study of medicine, eventually becoming a doctor, and Peter Frances Epps joined the ministry.

Despite the rigors of daily life, the harshness of extreme temperatures, the settlers had come home. They would establish roots that would take hold and flourish.

For David Shaklee, Iowa was the place for his calling. It was the source and the provider and would continue to be that for the Shaklee family—for many years.

Chapter IV

IT MIGHT appear, despite the rigors of frontier living, that life for the pioneers of Iowa was serene—and to a large extent it was. The Indians had been successfully removed West; counties were thriving. But, there were, nevertheless, some disturbing occurrences.

Of the Indian tribes who had been moved, Herb Hake tells us that the Fox had grown homesick for their prairies and bought some acres of land along the Iowa river in Tama County. The Sioux were trickling back in hunting parties, and whisky traders began plying them with liquor and taking their savings. In the early 1850's, a particularly unscrupulous whisky peddler sold a Sioux chief cheap whisky and, when he was drunk, stole his ponies. This led the Chief to tracking down the peddler in his home on the Des Moines river, and upon finding that he had escaped, the Chief beat the peddler's wife to death. The white couple's young son ran for help, but froze in the night. A year or so later, the whisky peddler avenged himself by shooting the Chief in the back and murdering all of his family, with the exception of two children who escaped and who reported the murders to the Chief's brother, Inkpaduta.

It was 1857 before Inkpaduta got his revenge. The area around Spirit Lake in the Northwest of the State was sparsely populated, the cabins separated by great distances. Inkpaduta and his men began a rampage of torture, killing and abduction in the lake area which ended in the murder of every family, over thirty settlers, and the capture of a fourteen-year-old girl who was later ransomed by Indians who were opposed to such behavior.

By the time a military relief expedition started out in pursuit of Inkpaduta, he was long gone and was never brought to justice. Although Carlisle in Warren County was a great distance from the Lake Region in Dickinson County, word of the massacre spread. Rachel Shaklee with three daughters whose ages were eleven, six and three, wondered uneasily if these raids would become a trend.[1]

In Southwest Iowa the "underground railroad," a secret overland route for runaway slaves from Missouri, was established, and here it was that John Brown, the abolitionist went into hiding. A free state, Iowa looked upon abolitionists as people who were meddling into affairs where they had no business. Clergymen, sensitive to the Mosaic Law, were the most ardent abolitionists and did much to aid and abet the runaway slaves. While we have no account of David's sentiments on the issue, it was, nonetheless, a troublesome one for Iowans.[2]

A settler's horse was his most valued possession and horse stealing became a rampant crime. Vigilance committees, who called themselves Regulators, went into action. As in most cases where justice is taken into the hands of individuals, overzealousness and personal vendettas were indulged in and, before the Regulators were disbanded, a great many innocent people were hanged on trumped-up charges.[3]

Then there was the War Between the States in 1860. A year earlier, David Overton had married his long-time sweetheart, Mary Goldsbury, and his old friend, David Shaklee, sold him half of his own holdings, some forty acres of land to cultivate as an apple orchard.

Enlistment in the Union Army from Iowa was brisk, in fact, Iowa contributed more troops in proportion to its population than any other state. One story has it that in order to qualify for the required height standards, David Overton, who was stocky and on the short side, stuffed his boots with newspaper. He was enlisted in Company B, 18th Iowa Infantry and served from Clarke County.

On the other hand, William George Sylvester Epps, of Southern origin, seems to have had no difficulty enlisting in Company G, 10th Iowa Infantry, while his brother, James

Edwin, who had remained in Tennessee, and who was married to Mary (Goldsbury) Overton's sister, had already distinguished himself as an officer in the Confederate Army.

Of the many Civil War stories about brother against brother, few are so compelling as the one Forrest Shaklee tells about David Overton, who would later become his maternal grandfather. Since no battles were actually fought in Iowa, although a Confederate guerilla raid from Missouri took place fairly late in the war, we cannot be sure of the locale of this drama. As his grandfather recounted it to him, Forrest Shaklee tells us that a rout of the Confederate Army had occurred. David and William George were assigned sharpshooter positions in a spreading tree in the path of the fleeing rebels. As the remnants of a Confederate battalion, led by an officer on horseback, came into a clearing, David raised his rifle, fixed his sights and fired a single shot. The horse reared, throwing the officer, while the men scattered and fled. David and William George waited in the tree to see if any of the rebel soldiers would return to help their leader. But, either the soldiers had assumed he was dead or, at that point, they simply lacked the spirit for another encounter. At any rate, they did not return. The officer lying on the ground stirred. It seemed only human to the two men hiding in the tree that they administer the coup de grace. Cautiously, they made their way to the fallen man, and, as William George aimed his rifle at the Southerner's head, the officer turned his face and William George found himself staring into the eyes of his brother.

Whatever dilemma may have existed in the minds of the two Union soldiers, it was erased by the stronger bond of kinship. Together they helped James Edwin mount his horse and accompanied him to the nearest Union Sanitary Commission. But, this episode, like all truths which by stretching credulity defy fiction, does not end there. While convalescing, James Edwin learned that his own son and namesake who had fought in the Union Army against the South, had fallen in battle. It was then that he decided to

41

defect to the North, which he did, eventually settling with his remaining family in Iowa.

Forrest Shaklee recalls that David Overton told him this story one day, while showing his grandson how to whittle a branch to a fine point. Apparently to spare her feelings, Mary Goldsbury Overton had never been told that her husband had almost killed her brother-in-law and that her brother-in-law had almost killed his own brother.

One cannot help but wonder about David's own feelings, since his younger brother Robert had enlisted in the army, only to die of disease eight months later in a Confederate prison camp in Missouri.

A year before the war, Rachel Shaklee had another daughter; during the war she gave birth to her first son, John, and a year after the war, her second, Robert Lenz, who was to become Forrest Shaklee's father. By then David and Mary Overton had begun producing their own brood. And, in 1869, Mary gave birth to a girl, Martha Jane. Three years later, David and Rachel's oldest daughter Margaret, married Christopher Columbus Epps, the son of Dr. John Winston Epps.

So it was that the families who had endured the rigors of pioneering, became entwined in common causes of belief and work and drew even more closely together through intermarriage.

The end of the Civil War and the advancement of railroads changed Iowa from a frontier state to one of stable production, with agriculture its key. New immigrants began making their home in the heartland of America, notably the Amana sect, who migrated from Buffalo, New York, and the Amish groups. Large numbers of Germans and Scandinavians as well as infiltrations of English, Welsh, Irish and Czechs and some Dutch immigrants who settled in Pella, contributed their cultures while adapting to American customs.

The establishment of railroad lines caused an old way of life to give in to a new. Wagon freight and travel gradually became eclipsed by the great steaming Iron Horse. In 1856, the first track from Davenport to Iowa City was laid. This brought about emotional reactions from wagoners and steamboat officials, but was greeted with great jubilation in the State capitol.

But, it was only after the War between the States that full lines were completed by four major companies. Where once bandits held up stagecoaches and wagons, the trains presented greater opportunities for derring-do.

One of Forrest Shaklee's early recollections is the tale his father Robert told him, of the bravado train robbery by no less an outlaw than Jesse James. The year was 1873, Robert Lenz Shaklee was only seven, but the name of Jesse James was already known to young and old. There was, in those time, a clear distinction between codes; black was black and white was white, and contrary to how he was later depicted, James was not thought of in frontier towns as a folk hero, but as a dangerous brigand wanted by the law. James and his gang learned that the Rock Island train would be carrying a large shipment of gold. Having surveyed the passage of the Rock Island train, James and his brother Frank severed the telegraph lines. They then posted themselves and their gang at a sharp curve in the track west of Adair County where the train normally slowed down. They had replaced the bolts from the fishplate on the tracks with rope. As the train reached the curve, the bandits, using the ropes, pulled the rail out of alignment and caused the engine to plunge into a ditch, killing the engineer. When Jesse and his gang climbed into the baggage car, they found that the gold had been delayed for a later shipment, so they robbed the terrified passengers of all their money and jewelry.

With the lines of communication cut, the outlaws were able to make their escape into Missouri, and the posse in hot pursuit, never caught up with them.

Adair County is roughly sixty miles west of Carlisle, and although James bragged that he never robbed a friend, a preacher, a Southerner or a widow, the residents of neighboring counties were badly shaken by the news of the daring raid. Apparently, James did not feel that the spoils he had gained were worth another risk, and he staged no repeat performances in Iowa.

The James gang was practically annihilated in a later Minnesota bank robbery and, with the price of $10,000 on their heads, Jesse and Frank James went into hiding. Jesse was later shot in the back by one of his own men and Frank surrendered to the law. By the time Forrest was a little boy, the legend of the James brothers had burgeoned into folk-hero worship. He recalls a jingle that children would sing:

> "Jesse had a wife
> She mourned all her life
> And three little children mighty brave
> But the dirty little coward
> Shot Mr. Howard
> and laid poor Jesse James in his grave."

Forrest Shaklee adds an interesting sidelight of his own. When he was about eight years old, his father decided to sell some farm land that he had acquired in Parsons, Kansas. Father and son made the journey together and when the papers had been signed, prepared to return home. Looking up at what seemed to be a fairly clear sky, Robert said that since it looked to him like rain, he might as well buy them some rubber galoshes, adding that he knew just the place to get them. They traveled a few miles out of Parsons, and came to a shoe store where the proprietor fitted Robert for the rubbers and seated Forrest on the glass showcase.

"And what is your name young man?" the store owner said, holding out his hand. "Forrest Clell Shaklee," said the boy, "and what's yours?" he asked in return.

"Frank James," replied the man. And indeed, twice acquitted in the courts, Frank James had retired from a life of crime to a peaceful existence in Missouri. For weeks, Forrest was the center of attention among his schoolmates as he told of shaking hands with the brother of the notorious Jesse James.

Chapter V

ROBERT LENZ grew tall and vigorous like his father David and, while he had a quiet respect for religion, he did not have the sacerdotalism needed to become a minister. But, he had inherited his father's love of the soil and developed into a capable farmer. As schoolmates, he and Martha Overton had become sweethearts. In 1887, when Robert was twenty and Martha, eighteen, they were married with his father, David, officiating. Two years later their first child was born. Ralph was a healthy and normal child. When Ralph was six Martha gave birth to her second son.

It was late November, icy winds were already blowing and the clouds hung black and mamiferous in the skies. The birth was prolonged and difficult and when the infant was finally delivered, it showed no signs of life. After repeated efforts to stimulate breathing by artificial respiration, the midwife made a hopeless gesture to Robert. He looked at the shriveled infant and it seemed no more than an inanimate sack of skin and bones.

For the young father, this was a twice-dealt blow. Aside of his immediate emotions of grief and disappointment, was another bitter realization. As a farmer he must look to robust and active sons to help with the planting and harvesting, to care for the livestock and repair and construct where necessary. Robert glanced at the cradle he had hewn and carved out of red cedar, and he made a decision. It was over three miles from the farm to Carlisle where there were doctors, and the hour was late. Robert saddled his horse and rode into the mounting storm. Of the four doctors practicing in and around Carlisle, Robert was able to rouse two. Normally doctors made their visits in horse-driven buggies or two-wheeled carts, but the stormy weather made the roads impassable for carriages of any sort, so the two doctors were obliged to accompany Robert on horseback.

Upon examining the child, their verdict was no more encouraging than that of the midwife. A general term for tuberculosis in those days was consumption, and that was the doctors' diagnosis. The infant had *consumption* and it was hopeless. When Martha Shaklee asked if she might nurse her child, it seemed the kindest thing to let her attempt to do so. Showing the first and very feeblest signs of life, the infant suckled and went into a deep sleep. The doctors termed the infant's condition, living death.

For weeks, even months, there were no palpable signs of improvement. Mabel Owens Shaffer tells us that, "neighborliness was fully cultivated and often meant mutual helpfulness in times of sickness, birth, death or other times of need. . ."[1] Although Rachel Shaklee gave what aid she could, she was quite old, Robert's sisters were married and most had moved away. Martha's mother, Mary Goldsbury, had died a few years earlier. So, the neighboring women came and took turns, helping with the chores, looking after brother Ralph, preparing meals and sitting with Martha. Although they tried to be tactful about the frail creature that lay motionless in his crib, Martha caught knowing glances, the exchanged looks and the whispered clucking to each other that this child could not possible survive.

Giving all the energy that a healthy infant might have converted to bawling, wriggling, exercising each of his limbs, the child named Forrest, lay in his crib performing just two functions: he observed and he thought. And, when the room was still of voices and empty of the bustle of people, gradually, very gradually he practiced with great concentration, just curling up the fingers of one hand and then the other. Later the child began to painfully raise an arm, then a leg. He could still not sit up, not even roll. After much practice, he finally managed to grip the railing of the crib, to raise and lower himself. Martha watched him continually and one day, when Forrest was about fifteen months old, he laid his hand on hers resting on the crib railing and said, "Mama."

46

Martha was so overcome with pent-up anxieties since his birth, that she fainted. But, for Robert this was a much hoped-for sign. Perhaps the child would evolve from his weakling state after all. Determined by this tiny signal to help Forrest develop into a normal youth, Robert decided to move the family to prairie land in Northern Iowa, but by then Martha was pregnant again and the travails of packing and moving would be too great a strain for her. So, it was after the birth of a daughter, Cecily, that Robert moved his family to a farm eleven miles west of Moorland.

Although he was little more than two years old at this time, Forrest recalls talk of this move and, in particular, a disconcerting statement that his father made. "We'll move to the plains, away from the smoke and soot of coal mines, where our boy will be able to enjoy Mother Nature's sunshine." He remembers being vaguely troubled by the words "Mother Nature." If Nature was mother, who was Martha? Could a child have two mothers?

Possibly these were the seedlings that contributed to a consciousness of Nature as the sole supplier; of Nature as a central intelligence which was to form the basis of Forrest's entire future.

Soon the child learned to move slowly, not at the vigorous pace of his brother Ralph, or even that of his younger sister. But, in his own fashion he learned to walk, to run and to rest in the prairie grass.

Robert and Martha kept in close touch with their parents. And, the grandfathers were influential in Forrest's early years. David Shaklee's ministerial talents were so highly regarded that in spite of the fact that he belonged to the Christian Church, he was asked to officiate as a preacher for the Methodist church as well as others. Little Forrest was taken to these sermons and he listened with awe as his grandfather thunderously delivered a point in the scriptures. David, who held himself somewhat aloof from children, fascinated Forrest. He watched the old man preparing for a sermon, the hair combed straight down under the preacher's hat, and the waist-length beard tossed over a shoulder as David carefully knotted his black string tie. To this day Forrest wonders why his grandfather was so meticulous with the tie which, for as long as he could remember, was always concealed by the beard.

When Forrest was three, Grandmother Rachel died. At the funeral services the little boy noticed that while there was much singing, his parents were weeping. He asked his mother why this was so and she explained that Grandma Rachel had gone to her reward. It was some time before Forrest could fully understand what appeared to be a contradiction. Without Rachel, David's zest for life gradually ebbed. A year later, at the age of seventy-four, he died suddenly.

Both the Indianola Herald and the Perry Advertiser carried the story briefly, "Father Shaklee died at the home of his daughter, Margaret, (Mrs. C.C. Epps) at Perry, Nov. 23. D.W. Shaklee resided at Sommerset, but had been visiting his daughter. He was buried at the North River Cemetery. . ."

Grandfather David Overton, widowed and remarried, did a great deal to fill the void left by his friend. Warm and jovial, and in contrast to David Shaklee, he thoroughly enjoyed the presence of children. Sensing this, they swarmed to him. But, Overton knew that Forrest was reticent and needed a special approach, so he engaged the boy's interest by teaching him new avenues of experience.

Overton was a hunter and trapper, and when Forrest was about seven years old and becoming sturdier, he engaged the boy by teaching him how to trap muskrat, raccoons, and squirrels. Pelt fetched from five cents for muskrat to twenty cents for raccoon. A natural frontier omniscience caused Forrest to learn very early that nature's balance depended on survival of the strong. Like all farm boys, he had no squeamish conflicts over the killing of animals, when he expected to eat them. But, unlike many, he did not kill for sport. The fur-bearing animals which he trapped, pelted

48

and sold, provided clothing. The game he hunted later provided food.

In late fall, when muskrats were furred out to their prime and when the creeks and swamps were frozen solid enough to carry their weight, Overton and his grandson would begin their trek. Muskrat houses, sometimes three to four feet in height were built by the animals with rushes. The old man and the boy each carried a spear which was used to flush the muskrats out of their houses, and as the muskrats swam near the frozen surface of the water, they were speared.

Overton showed Forrest how to skin the muskrat in two minutes while it was warm, throwing the pelt into a gunnysack game bag. Delay meant that the muskrat froze and skinning became clumsy and difficult.

Pete Cunningham, a neighboring cattle farmer had gopher problems. Besides destroying crops, the gopher holes created pitfalls for the horses: stumbling horses would often break their legs and have to be destroyed. More serious to the cattleman was a rider thrown from the falling horse and injured. Local farm boys were recruited into trapping gophers, and for each pair of front feet they submitted as evidence, they received ten cents. Young Forrest soon became quite adept at laying gopher traps. He would locate the holes and study the runways. Then, scraping through to the base of the runway, he'd lay the trap, fastening the trap chain to a nearby stake. He was always careful to wear gloves during this procedure, for gophers are quick to detect human scent.

After laying the trap, Forrest would scatter grass on top of it, placing an eight-inch shingle over the opening he had cut in the runway. Next, he sprinkled dirt over the shingle. This cut out any light and did not forewarn the gopher that his runway had been tampered with.

From initially being an indifferent farmer, David Overton had developed his acres into exceptional apple orchards. It was a source of great pleasure for him to conduct

Forrest through them, pointing out to him that the Red Delicious apples had originally been found near Peru, Iowa, southwest of Des Moines. In addition to these, were groves of Golden Delicious, Jonathan, Winesap, Duchess, Wealth and Northwestern Greening. For Forrest, reared on his father's farm of corn, oats, wheat, barley and flax, the orchards were a haven of serenity.

David Overton was something of a *raconteur*, and often when the outings were over, and they would rest under the branches of an apple tree, he would regale his admiring grandson with some tale of early frontier life. No doubt it was on one of these occasions that he told Forrest the Civil War anecdote.

Another story Forrest recalls has to do with the time David had been in the woods hunting when he was startled by the sound of a girl wailing. Following the sounds, he came upon an Indian maiden who had been climbing a tree. The girl's buckskin skirt had caught between the branches and was raised over her shoulders leaving her dangling and quite au natural. When the Indian girl realized the presence of the white trapper, she began an even more frantic screaming. David told Forrest that he was frankly stumped. To help the girl, he would have to lift her high enough to detach the skirt from the branches, but to lift her, he must raise her unclothed body. It was either that or let her hang there until another and perhaps less honorable trapper came along. So, he hoisted her until her arms were free to disentangle herself, which she did, screaming and screeching every inch of the way, and instantly upon being lowered, raced like a hare into the woods. Forrest still recalls the satisfaction he felt that, in spite of his youth, David Overton never treated him as less than fully mature.

The attention of his grandfathers had a beneficial influence on Forrest and may have been responsible for his often stated premise that he himself was never really young. His keen perceptions and inquisitive mind set him apart from the farm boys his own age, who were content to do their chores and play the rowdy games of boys. Brother

50

Ralph, with the typical impatience of the very young for ill health, ignored Forrest, and sister Cecily was still too little to be a companion.

But, essentially Forrest was a loner with nature. Lying in the prairie grass he learned about his wondrous new Mother. He observed how animals read the signs of Nature, where humans ignored them.

"Once while marveling at the formations of wild fowl overhead, I asked myself, 'What makes these geese, ducks, swans and cranes fly north in the spring?' I determined that they were guided by some unseen force, guided back to the place where they were born, their nesting place of the year before and years before that. . . .Then in the fall, without road maps, something—an inner consciousness—told them to fly south. That was the awakening of my relationship to Nature and I have since cultivated every thought that I could recognize as *my* Inner Consciousness."

From his mother and her friends, Forrest heard about folk remedies and became adept at identifying and collecting various mints such as ground ivy and catnip. He would pluck dandelion and chicory, curly dock, burgemont, joe pye weed, wild cherry, goldenrod and wild ginger. Some of these were used as vegetables or salads, some were brewed into herbal teas, others were used in liniments and others in medicine.

Nor was Robert remiss about being a companion to his son. Because of the boy's basic frailty, he knew that Forrest would all the more need to be inculcated into the manly arts. He wanted his son to become conversant with the sports that were common to the local boys.

Watching his son slowly respond and progress, Robert also understood that the time was not yet at hand. Although the tuberculosis seemed to have been arrested, still the boy was a mere shadow of his brother. Robert determined that he would dedicate himself to his son's total rehabilitation. But, even so, one day while watching Forrest resting in the tall prairie grass, his eyes closed, but apparently content, Robert realized that this son would never be a farmer.

51

Part II

YOUTH

Chapter VI

MUCH HAS been written on the difficulty of the farmer's life and, with its greater population of farmers, Iowa proved the rule. Because augmenting farm income had been, and remained, a way of life in the late nineties, after the town of Knierim in Calhoun County was platted, Robert Shaklee helped lay timber for it.

With land so cheap in the area, Robert was able to buy 160 acres about three miles south of Knierim, only forty acres of which had ever been plowed. He built a hilltop house, painted it white, and planted walnut trees that he had brought from Warren County. The black walnuts soon made a bushy wind shelter around the north and west side of the buildings.

Robert was one of the first in the County to raise Black Angus cattle. For range cattle, he traveled to West Iowa and Nebraska. Besides the Aberdeen Angus that he kept as breeding stock, Robert raised Herefords, crossbreeds for livestock, and pedigreed hogs, for which Iowa is justly famous.

Within eighteen months, the new town could boast a couple of general stores, two drug stores, three dealers in agricultural implements, two grain elevators, two lumber yards and a few smaller businesses. Situated on the Illinois Central Railroad in the Northern part of Greenfield Township and ten miles from Rockwell City, Knierim seemed to Robert an up-and-coming place for his children.

Forrest was about eight at the time of the move, and he quickly adjusted to the change. Here he was to spend more time with his father and here he was to experience a wider variety of activities.

Forrest's infancy on the plains had improved his health to the point that, while he was not stalwart, neither was he spindly. Robert was a firm believer in exercise. When he learned that Bernarr Macfadden, like Forrest, had been born "consumptive," Robert subscribed to his Physical Culture magazine. He was also an enthusiastic member of the local physical culture club.

From Macfadden's magazine, which had a section devoted to youngsters, Robert taught Forrest simple calesthenics, graduating to more energetic sports like boxing. The boy responded enthusiastically, with the same determination to surmount his frailty that he had shown from infancy. He tried; he learned and eventually, to Robert's surprise, became adept at throwing punches and improving his footwork. Forrest recalls his father's patience with him. "The gloves were bigger than my head and I would thrust and totter, losing my balance, but my father was always there to support me and we would work at it for long hours without him ever losing patience."

In 1904, Robert bought Forrest a copy of Macfadden's,[1] BUILDING OF VITAL POWER. In the preface Macfadden had written: "Without a normal degree of vital power, the attainment or retainment of health is impossible. Herein lies the close relation between physical culture and vitality, for the former is the parent of the latter by enabling all the organs of the body to perform their individual functions in that orderly fashion that Nature intended. . .when she designed them. . .Vitality is needed in every sphere of human effort. It imparts the power to *do* things. . ." Those words remained with Forrest.

Robert also encouraged Forrest's newly acquired hobby.

Collecting the bones of buffalo, oxen and horses who had died on the prairies, was a new and exciting project for Forrest. Each day, using the end-gate rod from a farm wagon, Forrest prospected for bones. Robert had allocated a space behind the machine shed for the bone collection, but he had not counted on his young son's zeal. The bones mounted. Skulls, thigh bones and ribs appeared in ever-increasing piles and began to take over the shed. Martha shook her head in consternation. At the rate that Forrest was uncovering bones, the house itself would not be big enough to accomodate them. Gently, but firmly Robert told Forrest that in his opinion the boy had more than an adequate collection and to please stop.

Forrest had begun to attend the Red Top schoolhouse, southeast of Knierim. While at school, he developed an ear for, and an interest in, music, and, after a year or so, he persuaded Martha to let him take violin lessons.

Albert Bakey, a farmer, was the local music teacher, and for beginners he was quite good. He taught Ralph to play the trombone, Forrest and another farm boy, O.B. Mitchell, who was called Obie, were his violin students. Three Adamson brothers were learning the clarinet, coronet and drums, while a seventh pupil was mastering the piano. Soon Bakey's students were making nice harmony and decided to organize an orchestra. But Bakey, knowing his limitations, told the boys that he had taken them as far as he could and that they really needed advanced training. The farmer knew of a music instructor, Professor Quist in Fort Dodge, whose orchestra had been awarded first prize in the St. Louis Exposition of 1904. If he could be persuaded to give the boys lessons. . .

Perhaps to make up for his small stature, Forrest was nothing if not plucky, and when the older boys set about arguing as to who should make the train ride to Fort Dodge some thirty miles from Knierim, Forrest volunteered. To the young boy, the Quist residence was imposing, and as he rang the doorbell, Forrest began to have misgivings. Mrs. Quist opened the door. She asked Forrest what he wanted and the boy explained his mission. Mrs. Quist, a motherly type, hesitated for a moment and then disappeared into the house. She returned shortly and ushered Forrest into Professor Quist's study. Forrest repeated his story, ending with the request that the professor come to Knierim once a week to teach the boys.

Forrest asked him just how much he would charge. Whereupon the Professor smiled and said, "Tell me son, is your mother a good cook?"

While he had not eaten at many tables other than hers, Forrest believed that his mother was the best cook in the world and he had no hesitation in saying so.

"Then it is arranged," said Professor Quist. "For a good meal of fried chicken, ears of corn and apple pie *plus* a night's lodging, I will come once a week to teach you."

Under Quist's weekly and strict guidance, the group began to take shape and, within a year the Professor told them that he thought they were ready to play as an orchestra. Requests for their music grew steadily and feet tapped at local dances to the tune of "Jenny Schodich" and other popular pieces of music. The orchestra was the most popular at square dances, and while he fiddled, Forrest learned to call the dances. Even today he chants in a melodious voice:

"Hop right up
and when you come down
Swing your honey
Go round and round
Allemande a right
Allemande a left
Hand over hand
And you go right and left
You swing her or she'll swing you
Go down the center and cast off two
Swing when you meet
Both head and feet

Head in the air
Feet on the floor
Go down the center
And cast off four. . ."[2]

But, the band was not allowed to play in the churches. Dancing was looked upon as improper and everyone *knew* that violins were the devil's instrument.

Although Obie Mitchell was first violinist, Forrest was sometimes asked to play either solo at parties or in duet with piano; and for this he was given the princely sum of five dollars. Forrest enjoyed playing in the group, but he was most eager for the solo requests because his objective was a bicycle. His father's farm income did not allow for such luxuries. Finally, Forrest was able to save enough money to buy his own bicycle. Working in his father's machine shop, Forrest constructed a bracket which was attached from the handlebars to the hub of the front wheel. Iron bands were fastened across the bracket to serve as a carrier.

No sooner had he done that, than Forrest realized that the bicycle could be used for more than personal transportation. Martha bartered fresh eggs for groceries at the general store. She was insistent that they be delivered while absolutely fresh. She had half a case, some twelve dozen eggs, which she wanted Forrest to take to George Potter, the store owner; Forrest was disinclined to hitch up the wagon and team and said that he would deliver the eggs on his bicycle.

By that time, the bicycle had become an extention of Forrest himself, and the townspeople knew he was dependable and willing. But, when it came to the fate of her half-case of eggs, Martha was skeptical. "You'll break every egg," she said. "I won't break one," Forrest promised cheerfully.

It so happened that at the general store, George Potter was discussing the exploits of young Forrest whom he considered a most enterprising youth. "Why it would no more surprise me to see that boy come around the bend on his bicycle carrying a cargo of eggs," Potter was saying, as Forrest hove into view doing exactly that, and, as he had predicted, without breaking one egg.

On the farm one lived off the land and on nature, so Robert gave Forrest a .22 calibre rifle. Although a shotgun would have been more appropriate for duck hunting, Robert felt that Forrest was still too young for the weapon. When duck hunting, Robert and Forrest would very carefully build their blinds, adding grass and rushes to the muskrat houses in the swamps. One particular swamp east of Knierim, which proved to be excellent for hunting ducks, Robert named, "Lake Michigan." The decoys were set in the water, and father and son would wait until they saw a flock of migrating ducks, then they would sound calls on their duck callers. These were made by filing down grass reeds which were encased in wooden pipes. Extreme care had to be taken so that the calls were invitational and did not mimic the warning sound of an alert duck. If the calls were sounded right, the flock would swoop over the decoys, at which point they would come within shooting range. The icy wind of winter guided the carcasses on the water towards the blind, and Bouncer, Forrest's dog, had to be restrained from swimming out to retrieve birds.

Wild geese and the now extinct sand-hill cranes were also part of the game hunted. The thigh portions of the cranes were excellent roasted and the carcasses, which were generally tough, were fed to the farm animals.

Forrest is careful to point out that the hunters only killed what they could eat. Hunted animals were never left in the swamps or the prairies to become carrion. In hunting, Forrest was again able to perceive how animals listened to the voice of nature. "She speaks constantly," he says, "not in audible utterances but the signs are plainly written in every living thing and even in the elements."

Many times their attempts to slip up on ducks were foiled by this voice of Nature.

Forrest describes a flock of ducks gathered at the edge of

a tule. "As the hunter stealthily approaches, a crow will suddenly fly off his perch, and swoop down over the ducks, cawing his warning to them."

"Or the hunter might be approaching a herd of deer grazing. The excited squawking of a jaybird communicates danger and the deer begin to slouch and slip away through the brush. Nature talks through the animals to each other," says Forrest.

Forrest observed too, how farm animals responded to weather signals. Long before there were any visible signs of an impending storm, mother hogs would gather corn husks and straw to make beds in their pen. "Animals watch for the signals and listen to the voice of Nature, while men have forgotten how to read or listen to them."

Forrest Shaklee credits what he has achieved to his instinct for hearing the voice of Nature. "Anything worthwhile that I have ever accomplished has been forced on me by the power of Nature. Like the animals I have always been attuned and waiting for the signs of Nature's revelations."

When Forrest received his rifle, Grandfather Overton made it his business to teach the boy marksmanship. Before very long, Forrest became a proficient rifle shot. Bouncer, was an excellent retriever, and the boy and his dog were inseparable companions.

When Robert was occupied with his farm chores, Forrest sometimes went hunting with a neighboring farm boy. One early morning they went hunting for ducks in "Lake Michigan." The tall reeds concealed the boys from each other as they carefully stalked the ducks, taking care to make no unnecessary sounds. Forrest was raising his rifle to fire when he heard the crack of a rifle and felt the violent impact of a bullet. He collapsed into the swamp. When his terrified friend rushed over to him, Forrest was lying in the swamp, a bemused smile on his face. A large brass button on his new denim jacket had arrested the bullet. It was lodged tightly in a bezel of brass. Martha was dismayed that the jacket she had worked on so diligently was all but ruined, and at the same time relieved that the handsome insignia buttons had been responsible for saving her son's life. For many years Forrest kept the bullet-encircled button as a lucky talisman.

Robert's Black Angus cattle were prized stock and represented his major investment. In the biting cold of winter, the cattle had to be herded into barns where they could keep warm. During a blizzard, the snowfall was so heavy that Robert strung wire between the cattle pens and the barns so that he and his sons could find their way and guide the animals to shelter. Forrest recalls a winter incident when he, his brother, and father were driving the cattle. All but one young heifer obediently made for the barns, but a strawstack diverted her and she broke loose. There was no time to pursue her, but as soon as the rest of the cattle were herded to the safety of the barn they went back for the heifer. In less than twenty minutes, the animal's limbs had frozen so that it could not walk, and within an hour it had died. "A sad example," says Forrest, "of an animal who would not listen to Nature's voice."

When Forrest relates these anecdotes of early life, the overall impression is of a sweetness and quietude, but underlying the stories is the basic harshness of farm life. The uncompromising reality of endless labor, sacrifice and a very real code of the land, which perhaps the following account will reveal.

Wolves roamed the prairies in packs, destroying much of the farmers' livestock. Principal victims were calves. A bounty was set on the wolves and the farm boys were expected to help thin out the packs. In the strange consequences of nature, Bouncer, a cattle dog and Forrest's constant companion, became mated with a she-wolf and joined her pack. Forrest was desolate. More than a hunting companion, Bouncer had become a means by which Forrest could relate to nature other than through human beings. It was not so much that the animal had learned, in the manner of dogs, to comprehend his master's thoughts and voice, but equally, that Forrest had learned to identify with his dog's spirit. The defection by his companion for a female dog would have been difficult enough for the boy to cope with, but that would have at least assured Bouncer's remaining with the family unit. The desertion to a female wolf identified Bouncer with the enemy. And, Forrest knew that when an animal turned wild there was no hope for reversal. Forrest was not surprised when the reports came back to him that his dog was among the raiding wolves. He understood the anger and bitterness of the farmers whose calves were ravaged. He knew what he must do.

After some time of tracking in the woods, Forrest discovered the whereabouts of the she-wolf's den. Early one morning he went to within fifty feet of the den and began whistling for Bouncer. At first there was no sound, but then he heard a stirring in the brush. Bouncer had heard his master's call, and now Forrest could see the dog. Bouncer hesitated, paw raised slightly, head cocked, listening. He whistled again and noticed that the she-wolf, partially concealed by the underbrush, was near Bouncer, but she was not venturing out. Another whistle, Bouncer whined uncertainly, still hesitating. Then, tail wagging, he trotted toward Forrest. A single shot in the stillness of the woods and the dog lay dead.

Forrest remembers thrashing through the woods home. He recalls that he flung his rifle on the porch and ran to his room. Somehow the words of his father telling him that he had done the right thing, were meaningless right then. It was close to midnight when he returned to the spot where Bouncer lay. The moon shone full and hard and he could hear the howling of the wolves uncomfortably close. Forrest worked fast digging up the earth with the shovel that he had brought with him. He laid Bouncer in a grave deep enough so that his body would not be devoured, covered it with earth and leaves, and with tears pouring down his cheeks, said goodbye to his friend.

Chapter VII

DESPITE ROBERT'S heavy work schedule, he was able to provide his sons with companionship and many diversions. In his mid-teens, Ralph, always independent, required less; Forrest remained Robert's special charge. As a charter member of the Knierim Physical Culture Club, Robert interested the boys in the art of fencing. Before long, Forrest became quite adroit at the art, learning to feint and parry, using his foils with dexterity. Fencing added grace to his already muscular physique. Although he wore the standard mask and gloves, and his foil was tipped with a protective button, Martha fretted that he would injure someone, or worse, become injured. He recalls in the early part of the century, several duels were fought, although these were, of course, illegal.

Nor would any rural scene in those times be complete without the precursor to Little League baseball. Robert organized what Forrest describes as a pickup team. Whichever neighborhood boy happened to have talent for pitching, was the pitcher; likewise, a good catcher became catcher for the team. When Forrest was the pitcher and Ralph the catcher, Robert was second baseman. Forrest developed an effective up-in-ball pitch which caused many of the players to strike out. He threw himself into the practice of pitching with the same totality that he did everything else, so that a muscular strain of the right arm resulted and has persisted to this day.

Because of the camaraderie of the Shaklee sons, Robert's interest in young people, and undoubtedly Martha's excellent baking, local farm boys clustered around the household on summer game days. Hard to resist as well, was Martha's popcorn. Edith Overton, wife of Martha's favorite brother, Eli, remembers large vats of freshly popped corn, drizzled with melted butter, placed on the porch. Edith recalls as well, Martha Jane's fondness for vivid colors. "At a picnic crowd you could always pick out Martha. You just had to look for the one in the brightest red dress," says Edith.

One frequent visitor to the Shaklee farm was Henry Wallace, publisher of *Wallace's Farmer*. His son Henry II was called "Harry," to distinguish him from his father Henry I, known fondly as Uncle Henry. The Wallace's family background tied in neatly with the skeins of most Iowa farming families. Like David Shaklee, Uncle Henry had been a preacher, but bickering between the churches, and ill health due to tuberculosis, discouraged him. Finally, his doctors gave him an ultimatum, "give up the ministry or prepare to die." Uncle Henry then joined the staff of a local paper with the ostensible purpose of writing on agricultural issues. Gradually his sense of reality and his convictions, led him to introduce political statements. He was soon obliged to join another paper. His interests in the politics of farming developed and was enhanced by his close friendship with "Tama" Jim Wilson and Seaman Asahel Knapp.[1]

Scots-born, Tama Jim Wilson, an assemblyman from Tama County and later U.S. Secretary of Agriculture, and Seaman Knapp, originally from upstate New York, had much in common with Uncle Henry Wallace. All three men, roughly the same age, were farmers but more than that, they were agriculturists; as a side-line each wrote on agriculture for a newspaper. Together, they helped form the Farmer's Protective, which Iowa farmers joined by the thousands. A fight began against eastern monopolies who were profiteering on barbed wire fencing sold to Iowa farmers. Tama Jim and Seaman Knapp encouraged Henry Wallace to branch out on his own agricultural paper and eventually "Wallace's Farmer" magazine was established.[2]

The "big three" in Iowa agriculture, Uncle Henry Wallace, Tama Jim Wilson and Knapp, resolved to do something about the poor quality of the land grant colleges in their territory. As a result of their work, agricultural education began to take shape in Iowa, notably at Iowa State

University at Ames, which nurtured the creative agricultural talent of George Washington Carver, among others.[3]

At the age of fifteen, Harry had joined his father in the publishing business. In the early nineteen hundreds, he was at the helm of "Wallace's Farmer."[4] This somewhat reticent, redheaded man, who was noted for being a better politican than either his father or his son, shared many similarities with Robert Shaklee. Both men were born in 1866; they were married within a year of each other and died a year apart. Both had religious and farming backgrounds. Wallace made it his business to visit local farms to keep abreast of the practical side of farming. Forrest recalls that he learned much about basic agriculture when he sat in on the two men's conversations, and remembers particularly, a discussion on tall, versus short, stalks of corn, and Robert declaring, "There's no money in the stalks."

Harry invariably brought along his son, Henry Agard Wallace, (Henry III) who was five years older than Forrest. Henry, it appears, was extremely opinionated and insisted on having his way in everything. This made baseball unbearable for Forrest, and he would attempt to make himself scarce, until Martha noticed what he was up to, and forced him in the name of good manners to return to the field. "There was," says Forrest, "no glimmer at that time of the man who would become so prominent politically, and in the field of agriculture." What appeared to be Henry's arrogance may have been due to the fact that at the age of sixteen, he had made quite a reputation for himself in the matter of grading corn. The opinion at that time, established by agriculturists in corn shows was based largely on the beauty of the ear and relied on such terms as virility, vigor and constitution, to judge an ear of corn. To young Henry, this did not make much sense, and in a five-acre test he proved that high yield was far more important than looks, summing it up characteristically with the comment, "What's looks to a hog?" This loudly touted effort became the basis for one of his first articles in "Wallace's Farmer."[5]

Throughout his life, Henry A. Wallace showed a keen interest in nutrition as combating disease, and one might have thought that this alone would have drawn Forrest to him. But, Henry's manner as a youth precluded that possibility, and while Forrest concedes that Henry made exceptional contributions with his development of hybrid corn, the two never became close.

Robert was an avid reader, in the main absorbing anything to do with agriculture. But, he subscribed as well to the "Philistine," a small magazine produced by Elbert Hubbard at his Roycroft Shops in Aurora, New York. If Robert was a dedicated reader, it must be said that Forrest was omniverous, consuming everything that he could lay his hands on, particularly Hubbard's "Little Journeys" and of course the monthly "Philistine." By 1905, when Hubbard's MESSAGE TO GARCIA swept the country with its success, Forrest was already entranced by what he calls, "the down to earth philosophy of Elbert Hubbard," and "the man who influenced my thinking more than anyone else." Little did he dream that in a few years he would become a close friend of the writer and pundit.

While Hubbard's trenchant and somewhat wry philosophy impressed the youth's thinking, the power and presence of another personality revealed for Forrest his own innate sense of showmanship. William Jennings Bryan, the man whose extraordinary eloquence catapulted him from obscure beginnings to a three-time candidate for the Presidency, and which made him Secretary of State, was, in tandem with Hubbard, the crucible for Forrest's intellectual awakening.

Robert's leanings towards literature, and learning in general, was part of a slowly engulfing wave that began to sweep the entire country and particularly the mid-west in the early part of the century. Foremost among the culture craze that descended upon the farmlands was the magical word, "Chautauqua."

The Chautauqua as an idea began as a place; an 18-mile long lake in New York State. Begun in 1873 as a summer school for religious lectures, the open air took hold and rapidly expanded as a moveable seat of learning throughout the country. By the end of the century, a number of entrepreneurs had stylized the basically simple concept to include the greatest talent and the widest variety of entertainment within the original parameters of open spaces, tents and lakes. In 1903, an ebullient pair of businessmen took over the lagging Redpath Lecture Agency. Redpath had previously been responsible for introducing such luminaries to the public as Charles Dickens, Emerson, and Mark Twain, but only within the environs of the formal lecture format; that is to say, in auditoriums, concert halls or opera houses.

And, it was the revitalized Redpath circuit which brought the Chautauqua to Iowa. In their book, WE CALLED IT CULTURE,[6] Victoria Case and Robert Ormond Case, describe the excitement engendered by this movement: Chautauqua had been promised for weeks, with window cards showing pictures of the Italian band, the buxom and ample-coiffed female lecturer, the prestidigitators, and David Roth, the man who remembered everything.

> "The buggies and automobiles and drays wore banners, 'The Chautauqua Is Coming.' The pennants fluttered along the business street, and the buttonhole tags said 'I'll be There.' The businessmen and the preachers held committee meetings every day, and the advance man walked fast and was introduced to everybody.
>
> "The kids scuffing in the hot dust at the edge of the cobblestones stopped to study a bit of pasteboard. It looked like a railway ticket to Omaha, punched and dated. They might be able to turn it in at the depot and get some cash. But when they picked it up and read the small type it said, 'You don't have to go to Omaha to hear something good. Come to

66

Chautauqua.' So they laid it back on the sidewalk and stood around to whoop with laughter whenever anybody picked it up.

"Now everybody was sure that the 'biggest and best' Chautauqua was actually coming, and they knew the advance man's name was Harold and he'd shake hands with everybody he met, even the same person a dozen times a day. Shake hands and grin and say, 'Things are coming fine.' All the stores had season tickets to sell, and the store owners watched a little anxiously, for they were all down on the guarantee and might have to dig into their pockets if the sales weren't good. Everybody who passed the ticket booths was ready to say, 'Yes, we already bought ours,' or 'I wonder how many are being sold.' The farmers fingered their wallets, looking at their pleading little wives, and finally laid down the money, as if they remembered how many hours in the hot sun it took to earn two dollars and a half. But there was something in the air—a sort of expectancy—that could not be denied.

"On Monday a couple of men went to work clearing away the junk. On Tuesday things really began to stir. There wasn't a boy in town who didn't know exactly which train would bring the Chautauqua car. They could wait at the lot to see it dumped there, or, if they were lucky, they might ride proud and grinning on the dray itself with the load. At the lot, the property men were pacing off the space for the tent. Another college fellow, in fancy gray trousers, was dropping tent pegs in a huge empty circle. Most of the women came past that block on their way shopping, not really looking, but seeing just the same. Then presently the dray came, with its heavy sweat-streaked horses clopping in the dust and the load piled high. The stuff went down on the ground in a pile of brown canvas and green-painted

67

boards, then the dray pulled off and went away for another load.

"It was blistering hot, but that didn't matter. The college fellow tossed off his hat and rolled his sleeves up. The tent was in several pieces, and when the dray came with the last load, everyone pitched in. Pretty soon the two big poles were pieced together and standing up, and the canvas was strung out on the ground. Then everyone pulled on the ropes, and up went the tent, flapping and jerking. It was then pegged out tight to make the top taut.

"The green-painted boards were being rushed inside to make seats, and with a great noise of pounding, when everybody started calling their boys home to dinner. By next morning everything was ready, with the seats in orderly rows and sections facing the rostrum, and the American flag draped above the platform so the speakers could point at it. A piano stood at one end of the platform, and a little table was set with a pitcher and glass ready for the ice water the speakers always wanted."

Young Forrest was among the boys, who watched the unloading as the Chautauqua tents were spread out between Knierim and Manson. Tickets were kept low in price to assure attendance. This was insisted upon by the performers, although some of the stellar attractions were very highly paid. College youths were the hired help, and this created an aura of tone among the backers as well as the mostly rural audience. In his book, THE STORY OF THE CHAUTAUQUA,[7] Jesse Lyman Hurlbut, D.D., tells us of one woman who said, "Chautauqua cured me of being a snob, for I found my waitress was a senior in college; the chambermaid had specialized in Greek; the porter taught languages in high school and the bellboy, to whom I'd been giving nickel tips was the son of a wealthy family in my own state who wanted a job to prove his prowess."

Audiences from the 1980s until the demise of
Chautuaqua in 1924, swallowed it whole; wanted it no other
way and indeed insisted that the program, content and spirit
be preserved intact for viewing by the next generation. Thus,
Chautauqua programs once proven successful were never
varied. In fact, performers were graded on their adherence to
the original presentation. As this movement became a national institution, rules emerged which governed the
Chautauqua. The Cases provide an example of the decorum
expected of performers:

> "Please do not perform free of charge at any social
> engagement in towns where you are scheduled.
> Please say only complimentary things of any hotel,
> town railroad, committee, superintendent, or
> anybody or anything. Please remember you are on a
> pedestal, advertised and looked up to in each
> community. Be dignified in greeting other
> performers whom you might meet on your trip. For
> one widely known person to shout, 'Hello, Bill,' to
> another, to slap another familiarly on the back, is
> usually against Chautauqua."[8]

Although Chautauqua had come a long way from its totally religious origins with a prodigious variety of subject
matter, including plays, inherent in every performance was
the requirement of a moral. Consequently, a pianist tinkling
away with some popular tune, was compelled at a given
point to stop and admonish the audience—"But remember,
all that glitters is not gold," or some equally incongruous
maxim.

What these performances must have represented for
sober-minded youths like Forrest, we can only guess. But,
given that he had never felt at home with childhood; had
from his beginnings identified not with his brother, but first
with one grandfather, then the other, and then his own

father, it does not take a great stretch of imagination to recognize what the impact on him would be upon listening to Russell Conwell present his famous "Acres of Diamonds," lecture.[9]

But, if there were some point where all the factors that had so far contributed to one being, became galvanized into realization of self, it was upon hearing William Jennings Bryan deliver his "Cross of Gold" speech. Originally presented at the Chicago National Convention in 1896 as Bryan's platform for bimetallism, the miracle of Bryan's voice, had in the early part of the century, reached a new peak of magnificence.

To this day, Forrest can recall his first glimpse of the person who was said to be "better known personally, than any man who lived in the first quarter of the century." The wrinkled alpaca suit, and broad sombrero of his first candidacy, had given way to a smart black tail coat, creased pants and a black slouch hat. He wore a low-cut vest on which was sported a handsome gold watchchain, but he never relinquished his trademark, the laydown collar and black string tie.

The man with the voice who was called, the "Silver Tongued Orator of the River Platte" took the farmlands by storm. Here was an ardent Democrat in country that had been avowedly Republican since the Civil War, when the Republican party was formed, and they idolized him, this man of the people; the Great Commoner. Understandably the following lines from his "Cross of Gold" speech issued in that magnetic voice, must have immeasurably moved the farmers of Iowa, Nebraska and Kansas.

> ". . .Ah my friends, we say not one word against those who live on the Atlantic Coast, but the hardy pioneers who have traveled all the dangers of the wilderness, who have made the desert to blossom like a rose—the pioneer away out there (pointing to the west), who rear their children near to Nature's heart, where they can mingle their voices with the

70

voices of birds—out there where they have erected schoolhouses for the education of their young, churches where they praise their Creator, and cemeteries where rest the ashes of their dead— these people, we say, are as deserving of the consideration of our party as any people in the country. . ."

And, later in the speech, "You come to us and tell us that the great cities are in favor of the gold standard; we reply that the great cities rest upon our broad and fertile prairies. Burn down your cities and leave our farms, and your cities will spring up again as if by magic; but destroy our farms and the grass will grow in the streets of every city in the country. . ."

And, finally with the characteristic Bryan gesture of outspread arms as though in benediction, the thundering final words of the "Cross of Gold."

Chautauqua had established a traditional salute for a particularly outstanding performance. This method of applause had originated many years earlier when a deaf-mute made a presentation, knowing that he could not hear applause, the audience waved their handkerchiefs. This salutation became reserved for only the most edifying performances. And, at Bryan's first Chautauqua in Iowa—the flutter of handkerchiefs was like the rush of a thousand bird wings.[10]

From his grandfather David, Forrest had learned the power of message, but Bryan's voice and his extraordinary presence taught Forrest the medium by which to convey the word. Although, what the *word* itself was for Forrest, he did not as yet fully comprehend. But, in the tall prairie grass he struck Bryan's posture and lifted his own voice in impersonation of the great orator.

". . .You shall not press down upon the brow of labor the crown of thorns, you shall not crucify mankind upon a cross of gold."

71

Chapter VIII

TO RURAL America, the Chautauqua was enlightenment, spirituality and culture. Some of the performers were imbued with a sense of mission, and for some it was a chore whose rewards hardly equalled the demanding schedule. Star attractions like Bryan, suffered the same inconveniences of travel and accommodations, but enjoyed national celebrity and were highly paid. Champion of the little people, Bryan became a millionaire through the Chautauqua circuit.

He was a dedicated and tireless performer who braved the elements, travelling by carriage, trains, and even on horseback to the remoter towns and villages. During his political campaigning, he spoke as many as sixty times a week to different audiences.

Born in Illinois, Bryan came from a sternly religious background. His father was a judge who believed firmly in the ethic of hard work. In the PEERLESS LEADER,[1] Paxton Hibben tells us that when Bryan was young his ambitions included being a farmer, a lawyer and a minister.

> "There was the physically pinched, emotionally stunted life of the farmer. Drudgery, William Jennings Bryan called it. . .And throughout. . .Illinois there were thousands of farmers, with the number growing daily, who for all their toil could boast of nothing better to live in than a miserable hovel. . .and nothing to look forward to but bankruptcy and the grave. It was a life to escape if he could, and with all his heart. . .Bryan wanted to escape it. He found a brief refuge in the emotionalism of religion only to learn that even for the converted, life went on much as before when the first flame had died down. . ."

Bryan chose to become a lawyer, but in so doing he did not turn his back on the farmer to pursue wealthy clients. He was looked upon as something of a maverick by his lawyer colleagues because he constantly championed the underdog. Nor did he ever tire of talking to farmers. And, although it was a life he had eschewed for himself, having witnessed the squalor on the farms in Illinois, he later tended to become rhapsodic about the Nebraska farm kitchens, which in THE COMMONER[2] Charles Morrow Wilson tells us he saw as:

> . . ."the provident throne room of the Great Plains domicile. He fondly remembered the unpainted walls kept bright with long strings of red peppers, and great bushes of drying seed corn and garlands made with dried husks of popcorn, with tiny ears peeping downward.
>
> "The food was in the pattern of an American epic. Venison was still plentiful, but to the delight of William, so were catfish, wild turkey, duck and quail. Upon occasion there was buffalo meat, juicy and lusty red. The perennial staples included dried beef, cornbread, jonnycake, flapjacks, and buckwheat cakes, all in prodigious abundance.
>
> "Grease lamps with cotton flannel wicks still lighted many prairie homes. Dried gourd dippers filled with dry corn or meal, beans or peas, and a score of other commodities adorned backwalls. Giant outside kettles, high windmills, lye barrels for use in making hominy and soap, all were among the accoutrements of backyards—as were the hollowed log watering troughs, and split-log racks."

A perquisite of the farmland circuit, was that the performer lived and boarded with selected farm families, and as such Bryan was a frequent guest of the Shaklee family.

Robert welcomed Bryan's visits and Martha was

flattered by his hearty appetite, (before the onset of diabetes, Bryan was inordinately fond of eating). Like other farmers, Robert was warmed by Bryan's interest in agrarian problems, and his loudly trumpeted faith was a comfortably familiar echo. But, staunchly Republican, Robert did not see eye to eye with Bryan the Democrat. He came upon Forrest practicing Bryan's speech and imitating his gestures. Abashed, Forrest said, "I wish I could speak like William Jennings Bryan." "It's all right for you to speak like he does," Robert cautioned, "but don't think like him!"

Forrest was understandably stirred by the dynamic speaker. Here was a man who embodied the qualities of religion, farm knowledge and brilliant oratory, yet he was nothing so mundane as a farmer or preacher, but instead, a world famous figure. Bryan's abstention from spirits was another bond between him and the dry states of the midwest. He told the story of a recent tour of the Orient where at a reception, Admiral Togo, hero of the Russo-Japanese war, was being toasted with sake. Bryan, of course, declined the Japanese rice wine, and when Togo persisted, said words to the effect that the admiral had won his great battle on the water and when he won a battle on wine, Bryan would toast him accordingly.[3]

Forrest recalls that this early earmark of the man who was to become the nation's most famous prohibitionist, exposed him to ridicule in 1913 when he became Secretary of State.

Bryan had campaigned tirelessly for Woodrow Wilson. As President, Wilson rewarded him with the Secretary of State post. The new Secretary asked the President if he would object to Bryan's maintenance of a no-alcohol policy at his own receptions. Bewildered, Wilson told him to suit his own conscience. At an official banquet, Bryan's able, devoted, but equally abstemious wife, Mamie, decided that a touch of color would look nice in the wine glasses and substituted grape juice. The newspapers had a field day with the story playing up Bryan's bumpkiness. Typically, manufacturers of soft drinks deluged Bryan's home with their products, including a concoction put up by an Atlanta chemist—called Coca-Cola, which Bryan considered particularly offensive. In truth, Bryan didn't even like grape juice.[4]

But, from the day he began his lectures in 1899 to the day he died in 1925, to the heartland of America Bryan was the Peerless Leader who could do no wrong.

During the first decade of the century, Forrest had many occasions to view this remarkable orator, witnessed time and again his spellbinding presentation of the "Prince of Peace" lecture, and was totally impressed by both the performer and the man.

In attempting to define Bryan's mystique, Forrest says that it was a combination of several factors. The voice was liquid and controlled, so that each nuance could not only be heard but, better still, felt. There was no depth, (unlike Forrest, who to this day has a remarkably deep resonance and timbre to his voice) but it was mellifluous.

In his book, THE COMMONER,[5] Charles Morrow Wilson has this to say:

> . . ."Fully aware that his voice could not be made "deep" (as later recordings proved, the Bryan voice was completely lacking in bass), he resigned himself to what elocutionists called, "natural intonation." And an impressive contrast of volume, from melodic murmurs to trumpeting shouts.
>
> "He was learning, as well, to look continuously at his audience ('their heads should move as the speaker's eyes move'), and was beginning to develop the use of the pause into a fine art. ('Pauses give your listeners time to catch up to absorb what you've been saying and to think for themselves, in case they wish to.') For good measure, he was making more effective use of his broad and quickly produced smile. 'People say,' he confided, 'that when I smile my mouth spreads out far enough for me to whisper

in my own ears. I think that's possibly an exaggeration. In any case, I've learned that when there's nothing better, and there rarely ever is, it's good to smile at your audience.' "

From Bryan, Forrest also learned the ability to laugh at himself and minimize his achievements, which can succeed only if the subject is entirely sincere in his humility. No matter what his political detractors may have said about Bryan, no one doubted his sincerity.

When Forrest was fifteen, his father decided to sell the farm in Knierim. Robert was forty and had worked hard all his life. Now he wanted a smaller farm with less responsibility. Ralph, twenty-one, would soon be on his own. Robert found his new home on eighty acres in the Madison County town of Patterson. Established by a man named Alexander Pattison, the name was misspelled when the plat was filed for record. However, Pattison continued to be an influential figure in the town's affairs. When Robert moved his family there around 1909, Patterson was a sleepy town with a relatively small population. The usual Iowan zeal for schools and churches was evident with a schoolhouse, and Methodist, Baptist, and Christian houses of worship.

Robert raised a few head of cattle, some corn and some small grain, and began supplementing his now considerably smaller income by part-time work with the Chicago Rock Island and Pacific Railroad.

For Martha, life was more leisurely, too. Now she could spend time with her relatives. Her brother Eli and his wife Edith, would sometimes come, in the company of Grandpa Overton and Martha Dunn, whom he had married four years after the death of Mary Goldsbury. Though in his seventies, David was still robust. On each visit he brought sacks of apples, the prize of his orchards. Since little went to waste in farm homes, these apples not immediately eaten or stored in the cellar, were dried for later use. If the days were clear, Martha, Edith and Grandma Overton would carefully peel and slice apples—spreading them on a clean sheet over a hayrack. To protect the apples from contamination, mosquito netting was laid over the fruit. Each night, down would come the netting, apples, and sheet, only to be reassembled the following day, until the apple slices were dry.

Each day the women took turns at cooking, which was more of a ritual of pride, rather than a chore. In farm life, even recreation had to be productive and on winter days, the women worked on quilting. Edith Overton remembers that she and Martha "pieced a lot," while Grandma Overton tended her vinegar pies, for which she was justly famed, or sat back in a rocker puffing at her white clay pipe.

When the men had returned from the fields and supper was over, there might be some entertainment. Forrest would oblige with a ditty or two on his violin. Ralph might be persuaded to perform a trombone solo, while Uncle Eli would certainly perform on the Jew's harp or the harmonica.

Forrest was still going to school, but he declined any assistance from Robert towards his education. Instead he hired on for summer months with Wiley Crawford, a horse breeder.

Wiley taught Forrest how to break horses to the saddle, and to train them in harness for a two-wheeled cart or for a buggy. Untrained horses of two-and-a-half or three years of age were hitched with a trained animal. The experienced horse taught the untrained ones how to pace. Forrest's own pony, Rowdy, was a farm animal who had never been trained to pace. One day, Wiley asked Forrest to go into town on an errand. Forrest decided to team Rowdy with a trained buggy colt. The colt immediately went into his pacing gait. Rowdy reared nervously at this unknown situation. A few soothing words from Forrest and the intelligent animal broke into a pacing gait as if he had done so all his life.

For two or three summers, Forrest worked for Wiley, while continuing his school studies. But, there was time for larking, too. Some of the local boys with whom Forrest had grown friendly, talked about a certain haunted tree in a

77

cemetery outside Patterson. It was said that everyday at dusk an apparition emerged from the tree snag making weird sounds. Forrest thought this was stuff and nonsense, and said so. At once the boys challenged him to investigate the ghost, if he dared. Naturally, Forrest dared.

Forrest remembers, as dusk approached one evening, the boys, about four of them, rode out in a buggy to the cemetery. When they had made sure that the place was deserted, Forrest and another lad who had elected to accompany him, scaled the cemetery fence, while the others remained in the roadway. Forrest picked up a heavy branch and approached the tree. He recalls that it was very still in the cemetery and, but for an eerie glowing of the rotten snag, it was totally dark. With a bravado that Forrest admits he did not feel, he marched up to the tree and hit it fiercely with the branch. Instantly and amid a shower of bright objects, a flowing white figure rose up from the tree into the sky making the most frightening and mournful sounds. Forrest stood transfixed. His companion had vaulted over the fence, and with the other boys fled in the buggy. By the time Forrest walked back to town, he had figured out the mystery of the sepulchre in the tree. It was no more than an old white owl roosting in the hollowed stump. The shower of brilliant objects were bits of bark which had become rotton and phosphorescent, known as fox-fire.

But, to the search group of concerned farmers, headed by Robert, to whom the boys had reported that Forrest had been killed by the tree ghost, Forrest merely smiled and said nothing.

Chapter IX

FORREST SHAKLEE was like a young river, energetic and raging to seek its own, and higher levels. Religion which had surrounded him from childhood, became melded into faith. Still a faith of denominations, and churches, and not yet the superconsciousness strongly identified with nature. It was to be some years before this comprehension of nature as the Creative Force and the sole supplier, became clearly isolated in his own mind.

Even then, like a clear spring, there began a washing away of staid postures and insularity, stimulated by the writings of Elbert Hubbard, and in the vehicle of message that he had learned from Bryan's oratory. Most of all, there was a driving curiosity that made the youth search and think.

Nor did Forrest neglect his pursuit of physical excellence. He maintained a vigorous regimen of exercise and bodily discipline. Bernarr Macfadden's "Physical Culture" magazine and his book, BUILDING OF VITAL POWER played quite as important a role in the youth's life as did his newer and more cerebral interests. He continued to be fascinated by the account he had read in an issue of "Physical Culture," about the man who had, from the babyhood of his son, raised the infant above his head with one arm. Year after year the man continued to raise the child even when the boy grew into manhood. This, Forrest asserts, may have been much like Macfadden's other vauntings. Nevertheless, as a youth, Forrest was sufficiently impressed by the account that he practiced this feat of strength whenever he could. Lacking an infant for his subject, Forrest would lift heavy farm loads or catch a calf and practice hoisting the animal above his head. Forrest explains that his was not so much a conscious effort to build his body, as a determination to achieve an immediate end. "I just figured out, I'm going to do it. And that was that. And I kept at *whatever* it was that I had set my mind to until I accomplished my purpose."

Learning that Macfadden was planning a national tour, Forrest wrote to his address in Physical Culture City, in New Jersey. He received a reply in which Bernarr stated that he would be in Des Moines on a given date and agreed to interview Forrest. The year was 1912 and what Forrest did not then know, was that the tour was Macfadden's last-ditch attempt to save his toppling "Physical Culture" and publishing empire. The sprawling Macfadden enterprises at that time consisted of his sanatoriums, one at Battle Creek, Michigan, another in Physical Culture City in New Jersey, and one in Chesam, England; an institute for Physical Culture Specialists in the New Jersey complex and his various publications, chief among which, were "Physical Culture Magazine" and "Beauty and Health," a magazine directed at women. Adverse publicity, culminating in the serialization in his magazine of a novel dealing with venereal disease, had brought the law down on him. It was an age when such topics were unmentionable, to say nothing of unprintable. He had been charged with sending obscene material through the mail, was arrested, and fined $2,000. Only the intervention of President Taft prevented his going to jail, and it was over thirty years before he was fully exonerated. A man far ahead of his times, Macfadden had among his believers some powerful and otherwise influential friends, among them the writer Upton Sinclair, who credited Macfadden's diet theories with giving him the impetus to write his famous novel, THE JUNGLE. At the point that Macfadden planned his national tour, he had been obliged to sign over his holdings to trusted colleagues.

Macfadden was then in his early forties. To Forrest, who was eighteen, the man in person was surprisingly small in stature. Bernarr stood five foot six inches in his stockinged feet, and these were size 5½. Undeniably, Forrest avers, he was dynamic, wiry and possessed of an extraordinary physique. His voice had a flat Missouri accent, which detractors have likened to the voice of W.C. Fields, (whom, incidentally Macfadden *never* thought was funny).

For his part, the former Missouri farm boy sensed in the Iowa farm boy a quality that exceeded physical attributes. In fact, Forrest may have served as a confirmation of Macfadden's oft-touted theory, that a muscular body assured a better brain.

Forrest was hired along with several other Iowa youths to assist Macfadden in his "displays" throughout midwestern cities. Five dollars seems to have been the magical fee in those pre-World War I days, and Forrest was to earn that sum, plus transportation to each city. Food and lodging would be provided under the ministrations of Macfadden's wife.

Marguerite Macfadden, who was as warm and welcoming as freshly baked bread, approached Macfadden's enforced disciplines with a humorous and almost tongue-in-cheek attitude. Forrest and the other boys capitulated to her forthrightness and motherly concerns for them. In fact, he says of her, that she was "like a second mother to us." On the other hand, Macfadden was a martinet on the subject of discipline. He had preconceived ideas on matters pertaining not only to body building, but to diet and life styles in general. A firm advocate of Horace Fletcher's principle of mastication, Macfadden insisted that Forrest and the other youths chew every morsel of the lusterless, but undoubtedly healthy food that Marguerite set before them, a minimum of thirty times. Forbidden from their diet were tea, coffee, cigarettes and, of course, alcohol. Raw vegetables, notably carrots, were the principle fare. Macfadden advocated eating grasses and was among the first to see benefits to be derived from clover and alfalfa.

Bernarr trained his young applicants rigorously. The boys were not hired on a permanent basis, but were to be on call when Macfadden presented his displays in each town. These demonstrations of physical prowess were intended to

81

spark up interests in his Institute's course in Physical Culture training, as well as to draw crowds to Macfadden's personal performance, usually presented in a local hall, theater or small opera house. Parades were held on the main street of each town, and consisted of a pride of muscular youths, some musicians, and a flatbed wagon pulled by an eight-horse team of dapple grays, (matched as well as possible, since the horses were rented, as needed, in each town). Regardless of weather, Bernarr insisted that the youths make their presentations wearing no more than breechclauts. "The pores of the body have to breathe and they can't breathe under wraps. Let your skin breathe!"

When enough of a crowd had been gathered around the flatbed, each of the youths was to exercise with a given piece of equipment. This was preceded by a discourse from Macfadden, extolling health through nature, diet and especially non-diet, (he tended to look upon fasting as a blanket cure-all) and, of course, strenuous exercise. He then demonstrated an example of his own estimable strength by tearing in two, two packs of playing cards with his bare hands in five seconds. This never failed to bring cheers and applause from the crowds, which consisted largely of women and girls.

Next, the youths, trying to conceal their shivering from the cold, performed their gymnastics using dumbbells or barbells. The exercises were the standard *jerks,* with one hand or two, or the *compound jerk; the one-hand* or *two-hand snatch*, with much attention being given to the bench-press, using increasingly heavy barbells. Before these public demonstrations, Macfadden was strict in his coaching. In detailing the basic elements of the *jerk,* he warned that two considerations must always be kept in mind. The first was balance. With the barbell raised above the head, the body must be directly under the weight. This he explained, meant that the center of gravity should be above a point midway between the two feet. The second consideration was dictated by the first, and it was that the weight lifter must keep his eye upon the weight at all times when it was above his shoulders. "Never for an instant take your eyes off the barbell,"[1] he cautioned.

Forrest soon learned that Bernarr was every bit as much, if not more, of a salesman as he was a physical culturist, and he was chagrined to discover that there was a streak of chicanery in the father of Physical Culture. The *piece-de-resistance* of these outdoor displays, was the lifting of an iron ball which appeared to weigh easily 500 pounds. Secured to the ball was a massive link chain, which one of the youths would grasp and which, with much concentration and apparent straining, he would raise gradually over his head. The crowds watching in awed silence at the beginning of the feat, would break into cheers and applause when the ball was finally raised. When it was his turn at the ball, Forrest discovered that lifting it was easily accomplished; the ball was hollow!

If it ever entered the minds of the townsfolk that there was anything spurious to these displays, they did not express it. While the young men watched enviously, some chewing at a blade of grass, some jocularly making light of the performer's efforts, the girls giggled in excitement or gasped in awe. But a few of the older women simply marched to the edge of the platform, where the youths were seated between performances, and tested their biceps, as though they were inspecting legs of ham. When questioned about this brazeness in an age of female modesty, Forrest says with a merry twinkle in his eye, that in spite of women's suffrage and female liberation which were to peak much later, there were always assertive women. To prove his memory, he sings a couplet from "Moonshine," a musical produced in 1905.

"I wonder if the ladies will powder and paint,
a hundred years from now.
To make them look like what they ain't
A hundred years from now.
There's no solution it's all evolution. . ."[2]

83

The parades held along the main streets of town in Iowa and neighboring states, Nebraska and Minneapolis attracted throngs of people, and Macfadden sold many of his Institute's courses to young men and women who aspired to follow in his footsteps. His spiel on selling the courses was direct; with an underlying promise of financial success. It was, he said "...the great beacon that lights the way toward your financial success and true happiness...Physical Culture is a living, forceful reality. Every University, College and private educational institution...is beginning to recognize its need ...Who is going to reap the rich financial harvest that is ripe for the reaper...competent to do this work?..." and on,...culminating with a facsimile of the Bernarr Macfadden Institute Certificate. This was handsomely engraved on a 16 x 12¼ sheet, with a medallion photo of Bernarr, flanked by two nude females and which was topped with the slogan, "WEAKNESS A CRIME." On one side of the certificate was a replica of Appollo Belvedere, while on the other, Venus disported demurely.[3] It was a very impressive document. Forrest toyed with the idea of signing up himself. Besides this temporary engagement with Macfadden, he had been working odd jobs and was saving towards college. He had an inchoate idea of pursuing some form of medical future, but in what capacity he had not yet decided.

In spite of the sense of revitalization which Bernarr imbued in his students, and the exhilaration of public performing, Forrest knew that this was not what he wanted for his whole life. Still he stayed with the parades and, whenever he received the summons from Macfadden, would catch the first train to join the group. He remembers Macfadden's personal performances as the ultimate in physical culture artistry.

In the sold-out halls or theaters, Macfadden presented a memorable show. He had developed a system of presentation which increased his stature on stage considerably. This method was simply to place himself on a darkened stage in front of a large open box covered with black velvet. Lighting was then skillfully adjusted to highlight his lightly powdered body, so that it seemed, from the audience to achieve massive proportions and greatly increased height. He was said to have learned this effective theatrical device from Sandow the Strong Man, when Macfadden had worked briefly as a stage hand for Florenz Ziegfeld. Under the beneficence of this lighting, the physical culturist adopted the classic poses of Praxiteles, *Narcissus,* of Giovanni De Bologna's *Flying Mercury.* All of which keyed his audience to a pitch of excitement, whereupon he walked to the center of the stage and lay flat on his back. A female assistant would then climb a five-foot ladder and after a great rolling of drums, jump on his stomach. At once Macfadden was up, bowing to the unrestrained applause of his audience.

But, it was at Macfadden's table, where the youths gathered after the parades, that Forrest grew to know him more intimately. With his young disciples around him, Macfadden discoursed on a wide variety of subjects, the root of which was always good health. And, good health could be maintained or restored only by rigorous exercise, regular fasting and a spartan diet. He waxed long and vehemently against the medical profession, claiming that drugs merely alleviated the symptoms of disease, masking the cause and doing nothing to cure. He felt that fear of illness was as deadly as the illness itself. Long before Franklin Delano Roosevelt made the words immortal, Bernarr Macfadden was saying, "There is no enemy to be feared so much as fear!" Heart disease, Bernarr was convinced, was due to eating improper foods. These, he itemized as white sugar, all products made with white flour, any preserved or pickled food, or those which contained an excess of salt. In spite of much of the jimcrackery of Bernarr's myriad theories on almost every topic, Forrest acknowledges that he had an early understanding of some basic nutritional values. His war against white flour, for example, led eventually to the widespread use of whole wheat flour. And his advocation of exercise for heart patients and fresh air for tubercular patients ultimately, came to be accepted. He was a total extremist in his views and many of his valuable theories were so mixed in with ludicrous advice, that although Macfadden went on to become a multimillionaire through his publishing ventures, he was always the butt of jokes.

At one of these sessions, Forrest listened to Bernarr's theories on health and medicine. Ultimately, he believed that the body must cure itself, and that it could only do so by Psycultopathic methods. In other words, his methods:

> "The secret of human strength and energy lies in the nervous system, the great central office represented by the spinal chord and brain serving as a storehouse. . .for the dynamic energy which is expressed through all the tissues and organs of the human system. . .We cannot presume to say what this mysterious force of life is. As we have previously stated, it is possible to diminish this energy by unwholesome habits and conditions of life and also to increase it by Psycultopathic methods. Whether this mysterious force of life is electricity or not, or whether it be a form of electrical energy, we at least know that it is not unlike electricity in many respects. We may call it nerve-force or vitality or electricity, or whatever we choose. We do not know just what it is, but we do know that it exists and there can be no longer any doubt that it is centered in the nervous system."[4]

Macfadden then used as an illustration the idea that mental concentration in muscular effort was another fact that should indicate source of energy. "Everyone knows that it is the man who can get his mind into his effort, who can accomplish the most in a. . .feat of strength. . .You do it by *putting your mind into your muscles.*"[5]

But, it was when Bernarr spoke about Nature that Forrest felt a strong kindling of recognition. In discussing the expenditure of energy by people with such diverse occupations as the clerk in the store, the bookkeeper, the housewife, the business executive, Bernarr acknowledged that Nature has the curative powers. "Nature has thoroughly provided for this natural recuperation...while sleeping and thus resting from all voluntary expenditure of nervous energy, the mysterious force that we call Life keeps up the involuntary action of the body, and also collects a new supply of reserve force ready for the work of another day."[6]

Macfadden left the midwest to continue his national tour, and the Physoculturist went out of Forrest's life; but many of his ideas remained with the youth. When, in 1914, the first of Bernarr's six volumes of the ENCYCLOPAEDIA OF PHYSICAL CULTURE, was published, Forrest began collecting the work. Today, he still has the complete set, as well as a 1904 edition of BUILDING OF VITAL POWER.

By 1913, Macfadden and Marguerite had come to a parting of the ways and Bernarr remarried. His bride, an English girl, was chosen from among five hundred contenders in a contest sponsored by Macfadden himself. Her title was "Great Britain's Perfect Woman." With Mary Williamson, Macfadden was to eventually build a multimillion-dollar publishing business, carrying the message of "Physical Culture" to its apogee. Always a publicity hound, Bernarr spent a fortune promoting himself and his ideas. He determined to be the first Physical Culture President of the United States. Because of the seemingly unlimited financial resources from his publications, Bernarr was abetted by many top government officials. His political acumen was nil. He endorsed Mussolini, and at one point hired a pro-Nazi editor for one of his journals. The father of "Physical Culture," who in his eighties was parachuting from aeroplanes in long red underwear, had become a national buffoon.

"He was a man," Forrest reminisces, "who could have, and should have been beautiful, but wasn't." Then he points to Chapter XX in Macfadden's ENCYCLOPAEDIA OF PHYSICAL CULTURE. The page is dog-eared and a quote from a doctor with whom Macfadden obviously agreed is italicized.

> "Besides these various direct practitioners of medicine, there is a large and intelligent class of physiologists, including the phrenologists, who nearly discard medicine, and, appealing to the laws of life established by the Creator, urge temperance in eating and drinking; exercise in the open air; securing of pure air by ventilating dwellings, schoolhouses, and churches; bathing in cold and warm waters; cheerfulness of mind; and the cultivation of the Christian virtues, as the only rational modes of securing health and life.
>
> "We confess we are inclined to forgive this class their error in banishing medicine, in view of their zeal and success in disseminating hygienic information of the utmost value and importance to mankind. *Put man into harmony with nature, and establish over him the empire of reason, and their theory would be excellent;* but as things are, medicines are 'necessary evils'."[7]

Chapter X

SOME TIME after Bernarr Macfadden had left Iowa, Forrest was scanning *The Indianola Record,* when he came upon an item that attracted his attention. It was an advertisement for a psychology lecture, to be followed with a demonstration of hypnosis. In those days psychology was looked upon with some skepticism, but since Forrest was of an inquiring nature, the promised demonstration of hypnosis intrigued him. He had read about Franz Anton Mesmer, and felt that properly applied, hypnosis might be of some value in helping the sick. The program given by a Professor Santinelli was scheduled to take place at a theater in Rock Island, Illinois.

Forrest took the train to Davenport and crossed the bridge into Rock Island. The theater was well attended and, as he had surmised, Forrest found the psychology lecture tedious. So, when Santinelli asked for a volunteer for his hypnosis feat, Forrest responded at once.

Santinelli made a great issue of putting Forrest into an hypnotic trance. Although Forrest was not hypnotized, he cooperated with the lecturer, looking blankly ahead of him as Santinelli passed his hand in front of his subject's unblinking eyes. Next, the lecturer commanded Forrest to place his arms over Santinelli's shoulder, then by sweeping him up by the legs, brought him to an upright position facing the vastly impressed audience. Forrest, of course, had realized at once that this feat depended entirely on balance and not strength, and that it was quite blatantly a trick. The device consisted simply of the subject placing all his weight between the neck and shoulder of the hypnotist. Thus, when the legs were pivoted over, the subject was carried by his own weight. Santenelli was so delighted with Forrest's resourcefulness, he proposed that the youth become his protégé for the rest of the tour. Since he was still saving for a career, Forrest agreed.

The circuit covered most of the larger cities and towns of Iowa. Each night, Forrest would act out the role of innocent volunteer, and the audience never failed to respond with great applause. But, the lead into the hypnotic act was always preceded by the long harangue on what Santinelli professed to be psychology, and Forrest fought off his boredom by allowing his mind to wander.

One night, a few months after he had begun his association with Santinelli, and as he was speculating on whether or not he had saved enough to quit the act, he was abruptly shaken out of his reverie by the sound of Santinelli pounding the table in front of him. The man was literally shouting these words, "What you think, you look. What you think, you do. What you think, you are!" Says Forrest, "Who would have guessed that out of a quaint show purporting to demonstrate hypnosis, these words would become the pattern for my life." Although this simple credo became expanded into a workable and living philosophy expressed in his book, REFLECTIONS ON A PHILOSOPHY, and in several collateral works, Forrest is careful to point up the exact meaning of the words. "I don't mean that everyone *is* what he thinks he is. But what he thinks, *that's* what he is."

Forrest returned to his family in Patterson. It was time for him to decide on a career; he knew that it would deal somehow with medicine. It seemed to the young man that being a doctor was the best avenue to treating patients on a natural basis. Naturopathic medicine emphasized assistance to Nature and included the use of natural medicine substances. Developing from folk remedies, naturopaths added manipulation by hand and later, electrical treatment. Homeopaths worked on the principle of treating disease with small amounts of like substances. Thousands of years before the birth of Christ, Chinese physicians gave their patients the dried-up scales of smallpox victims to sniff as protection against the disease. Samuel Hahneman, a German doctor born in 1755, was the first to give a name to the treating disease by similars, and to record that, by giving healthy people minute amounts of certain drugs, the symptoms of some diseases could be reproduced.

In more recent years, with the burgeoning of drugs, allopathic medicine was becoming the major form of treatment. Allopaths fight disease with remedies which produce effects different from those produced by the disease. In short; allopaths embrace all measures which they believe to have proven value in the treating of disease.

Forrest recalled Macfadden's lengthy discourses on medicine; a phrase had remained in his memory, "the secret of human power lies in the spinal chord, the brain and the nervous system generally." Macfadden had dealt more generously with chiropractors and osteopaths than allopathic doctors. It was not, however, the influence of the Physioculturist that shaped Forrest's determination to become a chiropractor, but something infinitely more personal.

He had not been home more than a week or two when he began to suffer severe abdominal and back pains. The doctors whom he finally consulted in Patterson and Indianola, were convinced that Forrest had appendicitis. Forrest remained convinced that he did not. Still, the pains grew steadily worse. Forrest made every effort to conceal his discomfort, but he could not deceive his parents for long. Finally, Robert had a discussion with him, in which Forrest insisted that he did not have faith in the general practitioners who had diagnosed his problem as appendicitis. He remembered that, when the family had lived in Knierim, there was a Doctor McGinnis who had befriended him, and whose practice was in Rockwell City. Dr. McGinnis was a chiropractor. To humor his usually compliant young son, Robert agreed to let Forrest make an appointment for Dr. McGinnis to examine him.

"And if he, too, says that you have appendicitis," Robert said, "what then?"

"Then I'll go under the knife," Forrest promised.

Dr. McGinnis found in examining Forrest, that there was a rotation of the second lumbar, in effect a subluxation. A subluxation indicates a vertebra out of normal position. This was causing pressure on the nerve of the lower right abdomen. Forrest responded readily to the treatment which was without drugs and, of course, without surgery. He did not have appendicitis—to this day he has his appendix.

Fascinated by the spinous and transverse method of treatment, Forrest began to learn about chiropractic. He discovered that it was founded by Daniel David Palmer, in 1895. Palmer, a transplanted Canadian, had founded a school of chiropractics in Davenport, Iowa. In his book, THE CHIROPRACTIC STORY,[1] Dr. Marcus Bach tells us that the term chiropractic stemmed from the Greek words *cheir,* meaning hand, and *praktikos* a word defining effective practice. Combined, the words simply mean hands, used effectively. Palmer discovered the spinous and transverse processes which he used as levers to adjust displaced vertebrae into their normal positions. As Marcus Bach explains it. . ."The basis of this new science contended that an adjustment releases nerve energy, gives nature its best chance to aid recovery, replaces osseous tissue and removes nerve pressure which is the cause of the disease. . ."[2]

In the first year of his practice, D.D. Palmer began to attract attention to his system of therapy. It came about when he adjusted a displaced vertebra in janitor, Harvey Lillard, who had been deaf for seventeen years. Lillard credited the adjustment for restoring his hearing.[3] Proceeding cautiously, Forrest visited the Palmer School of Chiropractic, on Brady Street, in Davenport. He remembers meeting D.D. Palmer, shortly before his death in 1913. He recalls the full grey beard, the slightly bulbous nose, the zealot's eyes, and most of all the sense of conviction in the man.

As part of a personally guided tour, Palmer showed Forrest his Osteological collection. In the main, the collection was comprised of rare spinal deformities, and was later added to by Palmer's son and grandson, and exists to this day. Forrest amused D.D. by telling him about his early interests in bone collecting and of his mother's fears that the bones would take over the house.

But, it was D.D.'s son and heir apparent, Joshua Bartlett Palmer, who most impressed young Forrest. Though he was only Forrest's senior by twelve years, B.J., as he was known, was a messianic and theatrical entity. Not a very tall man, with a Van Dyke beard, he had an imposing carriage, a commanding voice and a quick wit. He spoke in the imperial "we". At the age of twenty-four, B.J. had written and published the first treatise on chiropractic, proving himself a force of energy to be reckoned with. After his father's death, it was he who assumed the mantle to launch chiropractic to the world, and is quoted as saying, "I will sell chiropractic, serve chiropractic and save chiropractic, if it takes me twenty life-times to do it. I will promote it within the law, without the law, in keeping with the law or against the law...to get sick people well and keep the well from getting sick."[4] B.J. was clearly the challenging kind of man that Forrest admired; chiropractic seemed to be the right avenue for treating people on a drugless basis which was compatible with Forrest's feelings. The course on chiropractic was nine months. Forrest signed up.

Forrest admired B.J. Palmer for his brilliance and aggressiveness and agreed with many of his views. Among these was B.J.'s statement that

> "Chiropractic claimed to give nature a better chance in ways that I did not understand nor did my father.
> "Health does not come merely by taking medicine or structural adjustments...the individual must obey the laws of Nature to maintain or to regain health. Thus the present day patient expects to take his treatment, pay his bills, and be rewarded with health—which he will immediately begin to destroy

93

by the manner in which he continues to live. He does not expect his doctor to insist upon good posture, proper nutrition, exercise, fresh air, correct use of his body and mind at work and play."[5]

B.J. was a tough-minded businessman, with a flair for humor. Quotes were posted all over the school and ran to slogans like: "Early to bed and early to rise, work like hell and advertise." And, "Anything I do, you don't do is queer, Queer, isn't it?" In spite of his saying, "there is no greater virtue than adaptability and no worse sin than being governed by inflexible convictions," B.J. was rigid on the matter of Chiropractic. To him, it was the be-all and end-all of medicine. He had little use for anyone who strayed from the path of righteousness, as he saw it. He expressed contempt for the gaining reputation of Osteopathy. This constricted view bothered Forrest. It was plainly tunnel vision. He was convinced that Chiropractic was a long needed adjunct to the art of medicine, but he was equally of the opinion that it was not the only solution. He knew that no single health service did it all, and he planned for the future, a system that would embrace all proven medical services. But, he was wise enough to refrain from expressing his sentiments.

Once when Forrest was discussing Andrew Taylor Still, the father of Osteopathy, with B.J., and ventured the opinion that Osteopathy had not been worth a tinkers dam until the death of its founder, B.J. whirled angrily and said, "I suppose that's what you'll say about me, that Chiropractic wasn't worth anything until I died."

"You said it, B.J.," replied Forrest, "I didn't."

At the school Forrest was exposed to the Palmer philosophy of "Innate." Originally created by D.D. and perpetuated by his son, "Innate" postulates that the primal source of energy, or the vital force, is directed through the nervous system. In the Chiropractic Story, Marcus Bach defines it for us:

94

"...Innate was but another name for the spirit of life or God. Innate was that power which kept the complicated automatic system functioning. Innate was Infinite Life expressing itself through an individual for a specific period in time and space.

"D.D. Palmer had described Innate as 'a segment of that Intelligence which fills the universe.' He made a distinction between two manifestations of this Intelligence, referring to one as 'Educated' and to the other as 'Innate.' While these two manifestations were considered distinctive, they were also complementary. Educated Intelligence, according to the doctrine of chiropractic's founder, began with our physical life and ended with its death. It revealed itself through our sensory perceptions and was a conscious, mental function. Innate Intelligence on the other hand, existed before the physical body was born and continued after it was laid aside. It expressed itself through a spiritual force and was super-conscious. Educated Intelligence was limited, Innate Intelligence was unlimited. Educated Intelligence had to think and plan, Innate was intuitive, instinctive, immortal."[6]

" 'Educated Intelligence and Innate,' said D.D. Palmer, 'assist each other, more or less. At times they are antagonistic; Educated is concerned with acquired experience during life, and Innate with experience obtained during a period that is co-extensive with the existence of invertebrates.' "[7]

Forrest found this a fascinating theory and, in time, added to it his own conjecture of superconsciousness, as being one with Nature or God and which directed his actions.

"Innate," says Forrest, "did not take it far enough. Educated Intelligence is what we learn. Innate is quite simply, what we feel instinctively and intuitively and possibly

95

immortally. But there is an even higher intelligence, Creative Intelligence which is a gift from Nature. The gift of Creative Intelligence is the source of all knowledge. The expression of that Creative Intelligence is the Life Force. It reproduces, it heals itself, vibrating in harmony with the Creative Force—Nature!"

Grandfather David Overton.

(L. to R.) sister Cecily, mother Martha, a friend of the family, father Robert Lenz Shaklee, brother Ralph and Forrest Clell.

The dapper young Forrest with derby and without.

Aunt Catherine "Cassie" Shaklee and her husband Manual Milligan.

Uncle John Shaklee holding a relative's baby.

Martha Overton Shaklee and her brothers, Robert, John and Eli.

The farm near Mooreland where his parents took Forrest to be close to Mother Nature.

The young man as he looked when he learned the key to his philosophy at a hypnosis lecture in Rock Island, Illinois.

Forrest, the youth who developed an interest in physical culture.

99

William Jennings Bryan, the Peerless Leader. (courtesy Nebraska State Historical Society)

Bernarr Macfadden, the Father of Physical Culture. Forrest performed "feats of strength" in his touring group.

Elbert Hubbard. His down-to-earth wit and philosophy had a profound effect on Forrest Shaklee. (Courtesy of Wm. H. Wise & Co., Inc., Publishers.)

Grooming for a chiropractic career, 1915.

Recent photograph of Dr. Shaklee's first offices which occupied the upper floor of what is now the Union State Bank in Rockwell City.

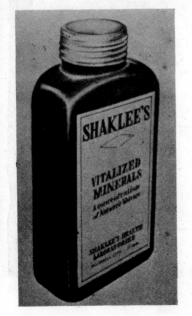

Vitalized Minerals. The birth of the Shaklee Dream.

101

Dr. Shaklee and Dr. B.J. Palmer for whom Forrest had named his plane at the Davenport Convention of Chiropractors in 1919.

Possibly the first doctor to make house calls by plane. Dr. Shaklee in dapper mufti, poses in front of his Curtiss plane.

Wife, Ruth, was drenched while christening the plane in front of over 3,000 spectators.

The house in Patterson where Robert and Martha
Shaklee retired.

Forrest, Jr. and Raleigh sport
with their puppies.

The distinguished Dr. Shaklee of
the Mason City Clinic.

Charles Lindbergh performed with the Selfridge Flyers in 1927 and, in a private moment, he flew Forrest Shaklee in his plane. (Courtesy of Culver Pictures, Inc.)

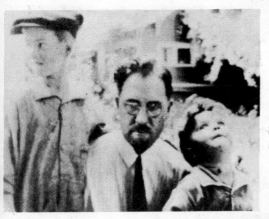

Despite a busy schedule, Dr. Shaklee spends time with his sons.

As Dr. Shaklee knew Thomas Edison, Harvey Firestone, and Henry Ford in Ft. Myers, Florida in 1929 when the three men were engaged in the process of chemurgy. (Courtesy of Thomas A. Edison Home, Fort Myers, Florida.)

Forrest, Jr. and Raleigh share their respective Army and Navy careers in a quiet moment with their Dad.

In practice in Oakland.

Dorothy Potter in an early glamour pose.

The young Canadian beauty was visiting the Bay area with her parents from Vancouver.

Dr. Shaklee and Dorothy pose at the ranch near Willits.

Camping on his own grounds.

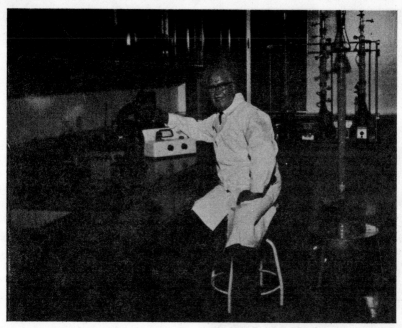

The lab beginnings of Shaklee Products.

The first downtown Oakland office of Shaklee Products.

The Forrest C. Shaklee, Jr. family. Forrest, Jr.,
Glenda and son, Cliff.

The Raleigh Shaklee family shown here (L. to R.)
Claire, Lee and Sandie, Rick, Laura and Karen.

Dr. Shaklee and Dorothy enjoy a quiet setting at home for their reflective hours.

Dr. Shaklee and Dorothy share a gala moment at a Shaklee Convention.

Dr. Shaklee in a jovial mood.

The William Jennings Bryan stance:
The voice of Forrest C. Shaklee, Sr.:
The message: "When Nature Speaks."

Part III

THE MAN

Chapter XI

THE YEAR was 1914. Forrest settled into modest bachelor digs in Davenport, Iowa and began his studies at Palmer. Certain associations offered small life insurance policies to young men, either already in business or still planning their careers. Forrest submitted his application to the Brotherhood of American Yeoman and was asked to undergo a physical examination. The physician who examined Forrest was Dr. Clarence T. Lindley. Upon entering Dr. Lindley's office, Forrest was amazed to find the walls from ceiling to floor covered with original paintings. In 1876, when Lindley was a medical student, he had been impressed with the paintings displayed at the Centennial Exposition in Philadelphia. Davenport at that time showed little interest in the arts, and the young physician determined to rectify that situation. His objective became to collect at least one piece of art from every important American artist. By the time he died in 1932, with the exception of only two artists he had realized this goal. Among the works hanging on his office walls were paintings by Gilbert Stuart and Winslow Homer. The total collection at the time of his death was valued at over $50,000, and was bequeathed to the Municipal Art Gallery of Davenport.

But, at the time that Forrest met him, Dr. Lindley in his late fifties, was still collecting. Every fee that he was paid became converted into art objects of one kind or another. In addition to his paintings, a unique collection of cameos and intaglios was also displayed. Perhaps what drew the older physician to Forrest, was the younger man's interest in Nature. Lindley had owned one of the finest collections of books on natural history, for which he was reputed to have refused an offer of $20,000. Instead, he had donated the books to the Iowa Soldier's Orphan Home, where they had subsequently been destroyed in a fire.

Rapport between the elderly doctor and the student of chiropractic grew to the point where they were soon fast friends. Dr. Lindley's home became the hub of Forrest's social life, and was, as well, an oasis for visiting celebrities. It was at Lindley's that Forrest met two men of totally opposite personality. The first was the long admired Elbert Hubbard; the second, a man about whom Forrest, at that time, knew little. His name was Clarence Darrow.

Hubbard, then fifty-nine, was at the peak of his career, but he was to drown on the Lusitania the following year. Hubbard's resemblance to William Jennings Bryan, which some of his biographers have noted, was strong enough to cause Forrest to make mental comparisons. The image of the boulevardier was there, with the long hair, flowing black tie, wide-brimmed hat at a rakish angle, and cape draped casually over the shoulders. He had Bryan's wide ingratiating smile, but with a wit and responsiveness unfettered by religious doctrine. He was, at once, accessible and human.

Hubbard was one of those extremely rare specimens who could combine the pragmatism of business with the headiness of art. He had been a free-lance reporter from the age of sixteen until at twenty-four, when he went into the sales and advertising end of a soap business. A year or so before Forrest was born, Hubbard, financially solvent, decided to resume his education. He enrolled as an undergraduate at Harvard. This experience was incompatible with a man of thirty-nine, and left him thereafter somewhat soured on formal education. He decided to return to writing, but was not satisfied with merely expressing views. He became a printer and craftsman. The seat of these endeavors was the Roycroft Shops which he founded in East Aurora, a suburb of Buffalo, New York. Patterned after the style of William Morris in England and named for the seventeenth century English printers, Thomas and Samuel Roycroft, the Roycrofters printed periodicals and books and manufactured artifacts. All this, of course, under the unflagging supervision of Fra Elbert, as he called himself.

In 1895, Hubbard wrote and published the first of his "Little Journeys," a pamphlet on George Eliot. His homespun approach to great lives became increasingly popular, and the "Little Journeys" included a series on philosophers and statesmen, as well as businessmen. He then began a periodical called the "Philistine." At first he enlisted the support of contributors, among whom, was Steven Crane, but four years later decided to write every word of each issue himself. Circulation grew phenomenally, particularly after the publication of his short essay, A MESSAGE TO GARCIA, in an 1899 issue of the "Philistine." This tract, which actually had nothing to do with the Cuban General Garcia, but dealt with work efficiency, became a minor bible of business philosophy. According to the foreword, printed in a later edition, A MESSAGE TO GARCIA sold 40,000,000 copies and during their war of 1904, was printed in both Japanese and Russian. Hubbard was, in a sense, the vanguard of the paperback books which emerged during World War II. Not until his publications had there ever been such a proliferation of books or such widespread interest in reading. He was, in himself and his works, the Chautauqua of literature.

Hubbard's personal life became chaotic at this point. His first marriage collapsed in scandal in 1903 when it was revealed that he had been having a liaison with a writer, Alice Moore, whom he married the following year.

Each May to September, Hubbard joined the talented speakers who lectured throughout the country. He who had single-handedly popularized literature, was now entering the realm of personal appearances, and he did so with the same panache with which he wrote.

Dr. Lindley's round table conferences with Hubbard, Darrow, and Forrest, occurred at the close of the doctor's office day around six p.m. and went on late into the night. Forrest was greatly flattered at being included in these sessions for, just as Emerson and Ingersoll were Hubbard's early idols, Elbert became his. He recalls their many discussions both at Dr. Lindley's table, on outings that he and the philosopher took and on a visit that he made at Hubbard's invitation to the Roycroft Shops in East Aurora.

It was at Roycroft that Forrest saw Elbert for the last time before the writer's fateful voyage. It was there that he dedicated a complete set of his "Little Journeys" to Forrest, and unwinding the flowing black scarf which he wore tied at the throat, presented it to Forrest as a keepsake. Forrest remembers gems of conversation that Hubbard tossed off, many of which he recognized as quotes from the ROYCROFT DICTIONARY[1] or THE NOTEBOOK OF ELBERT HUBBARD, but as Forrest says, "How those sayings come to life when expressed by their creator." Hubbard's pearls of wisdom encompassed a myriad of subjects. He could, in the same vein, tackle justice, criminality, jury and government, and he had a precise definition for each. Hubbard viewed justice as "a system of revenge where the State imitates the criminal." And, a criminal, he defined as "one who does by illegal means what all the rest of us do legally." The jury that reached verdicts he dismissed as, "the humble apology of Civilization to Savagery." And, government, he saw as "a kind of legalized pillage." More realist than cynic, Hubbard declared that a person's back was "that part of his body to which his friend directs his remarks when he tells him the truth." A brain, he said, was "a commodity as scarce as radium and more precious. . ."

Nor was any subject too sacred to escape his scalpel wit. Religion in his lexicon was merely "philosophy touched with emotion." Piety was dismissed as "the tinfoil of pretence. That feeling of reverence that we have toward the Almighty on account of his supposed resemblance to ourselves." A doubter was simply "a good-for-nothing who does not knock before entering the bathroom of the Faithful." Charity, Hubbard maintained was, "a thing that begins at home and usually stays there." Church unity he defined as, "going to my church." On the other hand, "An atheist," Hubbard said, was "any man who does not believe in himself."

The man for whom work was a great restorative, had no patience for idlers. Boredom, claimed Hubbard, was "a period of rest between I did and I will. . ." He created a parable on the subject of Boredom which stated that, "the word Boredom comes from Bore, a tired son of Noah. After the subsidence of the waters, Bore wandered about the earth, yawning and gaping and stretching, for at that time malaria oozed from many stagnant pools. Finally, absolutely exhausted, Bore being afraid to lie down on the damp and slimy soil, rested on the seventh day on his own bean, hence boredom." But work, that he described as, "a plan of God to circumvent the Devil" and "that which keeps us out of trouble."

Nature, Forrest's Godhead, had many interpretations from Hubbard. She was first, "the Unseen Intelligence which loved us into being, and is disposing of us by the same token. Nature was that which everyone but a theologian understands, but which no one can define."

Then, there was Clarence Darrow. Never before had Forrest met anyone of such adamantine brilliance. In contrast to Bryan's pietistic oratory, or Hubbard's wry optimism, Darrow was a seeker of truth who lay bare sentimentality and banished myths.

At the time that Hubbard, Darrow, and Forrest met at Dr. Lindley's, Darrow, a couple of years younger than Hubbard, was already a famous lawyer.

Born of humble, but well-educated parents, in Kinsman, Ohio, Darrow grew up in an environment of learning. His father was an idealist who, by reading, sought refuge from the realities of his trade, (he was a furniture maker and undertaker). Darrow's mother was pragmatic, but intelligent as well as industrious. His parents supported such unpopular causes as women's rights, and were champions of the oppressed. Darrow grew up learning to question incisively. This gift became honed to the point where, for Darrow, to challenge was as natural as breathing. He had strong opinions which were usually counter to those of his times.[2]

With the sense not so much of awe, but of the fact that he was in the presence of extraordinary thinkers, Forrest, a silent auditor, listened to the views expressed by Hubbard and Darrow. Dr. Lindley, who provided the forum, was friendly arbiter when opinions clashed, and always the genial host. Hubbard and Darrow were in agreement on the subject of education. "A college," said Hubbard, was "a place where you have to go in order to find out there is nothing in it." And, universities, he thought, "were institutions for the prevention of learning." "A teacher," said Elbert, "was a person. . .who instills in the head of another person, either voluntarily or for pay, the sum and substance of his. . .ignorance." Whereas a scholar, according to Hubbard, was either "an ornate fossil. . .a man long on advice but short on action, who thinks he thinks." Or, "One who draws his breath—and salary. . ."

Darrow's views, though less ascerbic, were in accord. Said he of his days at the district school and the academy, ". . .I cannot avoid a feeling of the appalling waste of time. Never since those days have I had occasion to use much of the arithmetic that I learned. . .This is the experience of almost all the boys and girls who went to school when I was young; and. . .this is true today."[3]

Typically, Darrow went on from arithmetic to point out the flaws in teaching grammar, pronounciation and language in general. History was likewise of no avail. "What purpose did it serve to learn the names of presidents, kings, and chiefs of war and those accidents that had been accepted as great events of the world—none of it having any relationship to our lives. . . ?"[4] Darrow repeated these thoughts when he set them down in his autobiography, MY LIFE. "In youth, and probably in later life, everything back of our own existence seems weird and unreal and far removed from the life we know. Attempting to store the brain with unrelated facts and matters entirely irrelevant to the present is worse than useless, for it confuses and distorts."[5]

"History," claimed Elbert, with some complacency, having popularized it in his "Little Journeys," "is gossip well told."

Shades of Darrow's impatience with restrictions on freedom imposed by schooling are evinced by these thoughts. "Schools were not established to teach and encourage the pupil to think; beyond furnishing a place for keeping children out of the way. . .the teachers were employed to teach the truth, and the most important truths concerned the salvation of their souls. From the first grade to the end of college. . .they were taught not to think and the instructor who dared to utter anything in conflict with ordinary beliefs and customs was promptly dismissed if not destroyed. . ."[6] It is easy to understand, in view of these sentiments, why Darrow championed the cause of teacher John Scopes, ten years later.

Forrest, on the brink of a medical career, listened raptly as Darrow took apart various institutions beginning with the bar association, whom he claimed, "lay down every conceivable condition; require a longer preliminary study and exact a college education and long courses in law schools, to keep new members out of the closed circle. The Lawyer's Union is about as anxious to encourage competition as the Plumber's Union. . .or the United States Steel Co., or the American Medical Association." Mention of the latter, brought about some good-natured needling from Hubbard. "A doctor," he said, "was a person who has taken seriously the biblical injunction, 'Physician *heel* thyself ! '"[7]

To which Darrow added that it was Shakespeare who had said "Kill all the doctors." Whereupon Forrest noted that

Voltaire had suggested all doctors be strung up using the entrails of lawyers. Darrow, whose parents had steeped him in the works of Jefferson, Voltaire, and Paine, chuckled.

"Ah yes, a lawyer," smiled Hubbard, "is a person who takes *this* from *that,* with the result that *That* has not where to lay his head. Lawyers are the only men in whom ignorance is not punished."

Hubbard continued his tour, leaving Iowa and the round table group discussions, which Darrow continued intermittently. Forrest plunged into his work at the school observing the techniques of B.J. Palmer and studying the then new diagnostic technique of x-ray. Like most of the students, he became mildly enamored with B.J.'s wife, Mabel. Herself a former student and then a chiropractor, Mabel was the helm from which the students perceived their horizons. She was, as well, anchor to her audacious and dedicated husband.

It was inevitable for Forrest and Darrow, at some point, to discuss William Jennings Bryan. Darrow had known Bryan from the days of his first nomination in 1896. With his friend, Governor Altgeld of Illinois, Darrow had been in the audience when Bryan electrified it with his Cross of Gold speech. Darrow and Altgeld agreed wholeheartedly with Bryan's Free Silver Platform and, when he won the Democratic nomination, threw their hats in with him. They were defeated by McKinley. Conceding that Bryan was the most captivating speaker he had ever heard, Darrow had doubts about his ability as a politician. He recalled that appraising Bryan's Chicago Convention triumph, Altgeld had said to him on the following day, "I've been thinking over Bryan's speech. What did he say anyhow?"[8]

In 1900 when Bryan was nominated, Darrow supported him again. The Nebraskan was defeated by a larger majority than before. Finally, in 1908 upon Bryan's third and final nomination for the Presidency, Darrow felt that he had followed Bryan long enough and refused to campaign for him.

Ultimately, Darrow was to become Bryan's adversary and nemesis.

Bryan was now Secretary of State and he was embarrassing Woodrow Wilson with his anti-war sentiments. He was also continuing his beloved Chautauqua circuit, which drew criticism upon him from the press. To charges that he was earning a handsome salary of $12,000 a year, Bryan countered that he had sacrificed $40,000 in lecture earnings campaigning for Wilson. Darrow considered Bryan, with his fundamentalist principles, a narrow man. Conceding that Bryan was true to the cause of the people as he understood political and social views, he was, in Darrow's opinion, stubbornly righteous. "He never cared to read, much less study; he knew, without investigation or thought."[9] Forrest, remembering the grandiloquence of the Silver Tongued Orator, was irked by Darrow's parsimonious evaluation of his idol. But, perhaps more than anything else, what antagonized Forrest towards the attorney was Darrow's contempt for his most sacred trust, Nature.

In MY LIFE, written some twenty years later, Darrow expounds on these sentiments:

"I grew weary of. . .everlasting talk of 'natural rights' . . .if natural rights means anything, it means that the individual rights are rights in the sense of human conception. Nothing is so cruel, so wanton, so unfeeling as Nature; she moves with the weight of a glacier carrying everything before her. In the eyes of Nature, neither man nor any of the other animals mean anything whatever. The rock-ribbed mountains, the tempestuous sea, the scorching desert, the myriad weeds and insects and wild beasts that infest the earth, and the noblest man, are all one. Each and all are helpless against the cruelty and immutability of the resistless processes of Nature. . . .Nowhere in Nature is there the slightest evidence of kindness and consideration, or a feeling for the suffering and the weak, except in the narrow circle of brief family life. . ."[10]

Appalled, the twenty-one year old student attempted to parry with the master dissector, but, Forrest admits that Darrow's ability to reduce and dissolve any argument was beyond him.

It was the Spring of 1915 and Forrest was to graduate from Palmer in June. In May, while he was working on his finals, the newspapers headlined the sinking of the Lusitania off the coast of Ireland. The ship carrying 1,700 passengers had also been stocked with munitions. The Germans had warned the steamship line that they would torpedo any vessels carrying arms to England. On the early morning of May 7th, they torpedoed the Lusitania. Among those drowned were Elbert Hubbard and his wife Alice.

Alone in his room, Forrest wound the black silk tie given him in token of friendship by the writer, and remembered one of Hubbard's most poignant definitions. "A friend," said Hubbard, "is a masterpiece of Nature."

Chapter XII

THE TIME Forrest spent in Davenport was significant for several reasons. First, he was on track to a career; then there was the stimulation of the meetings with Hubbard and Darrow; and, finally, he became awakened for the first time to love.

The object of his affections was Ruth Chapin, and the manner in which the student and girl met has the quaint charm of a tintype. Forrest had been teaching a Sunday School Class with a group called the Christian Endeavour. A picnic had been planned by the group and a casual friend named Walter, asked Forrest to join him and two girls at the Watch Tower Park in Rock Island.

Ruth Chapin and her sister Florence were waiting for the young men at the Park. The girls had each prepared a picnic hamper to share with their escorts. The sisters were accountants. Florence, the older of the two, was head auditor for Crown Overall and Shirt Factory; Ruth held a less exalted position, keeping books for a clothing manufacturer. Florence was bright and independent, and typified the saying of those days, that she was too smart for most men. Ruth, while intelligent, was vivacious and in no way threatening. Walter had very obviously taken a shine to Ruth and, since the sisters were inseparable, he had arranged for Florence to be Forrest's blind date.

When it was time to proceed to the picnic grounds, Forrest picked up the hamper that Ruth had prepared and she linked her arm in his.

Walter was then obliged to escort Florence. In a moment when he could take Forrest aside, Walter muttered angrily, "You're double-crossing me."

"Good," said Forrest.

From that budding, the romance blossomed and a wedding date was set for December. What time could be spared from his studies at Palmer, Forrest spent in simple and necessarily inexpensive entertainment with Ruth. They went for strolls and listened to the band in the park, and, when he could manage it, went to that fascinating new entertainment, the moving pictures, where they roared over the antics of Chaplin, Mabel Norman, and Marie Dressler, or caught their breath over the hazards of Pearl White in her serialized, "Perils of Pauline."

On one such outing, as they were returning on the streetcar, Ruth ran into a girlfriend whom she had not seen since their school days. Proudly she introduced her fiance. It was a hot summer evening, the streetcar windows were open, and Ruth's chum expressed a desire for popcorn. Aware that he was spending the nickel that was meant to get him home from Ruth's residence, Forrest gallantly bought popcorn for the girls from a street vendor.

It was late by the time Forrest had seen Ruth home and began the long trek to his own quarters across town. He took a shortcut through a little wooded swale walking cautiously in the dark. All at once, what had seemed to be a tree snag, moved towards him and Forrest found himself staring into the mouth of a .38 caliber pistol. The situation struck Forrest as so ludicrous, that he began to laugh uncontrollably.

"This is no laughing matter," snapped the man behind the .38. "This is a stick-up!"

"It's a laughing matter to me," said Forrest, thinking of his last nickel and the popcorn. "I'm broke."

The man switched on a flashlight and taking in Forrest's neat appearance from the smart derby to his polished shoes, said flatly, "I don't believe you have no money."

"You can search me," Forrest replied, "but who in his right mind would risk breaking his neck in these Godforsaken woods if he had a nickel for the streetcar?"

The man thought briefly, then nodded and disappeared as he had come. Reflecting on that incident, Forrest chuckles. "He let me go unharmed because I simply appealed to that most uncommon quality, common sense."

By the time he graduated from Palmer that June, Forrest had a clear picture of what he wanted from his training. Essentially, he expected to remain Naturopathic in his treatment of patients, but he did not have a closed-mind regarding total medical services. At Palmer, Forrest had become more than ever convinced that poor nutrition was an important cause of *dis*-ease, as Chiropractic termed it. He saw undernourished patients as well as overfed patients, who suffered from improper nutrition. The subject engaged his interest almost completely.

On a visit to his parents, he decided to call on Dr. McGinnis who had previously treated him. He found the Rockwell City chiropractor in a state of personal turmoil. He and his wife were getting divorced, and McGinnis wanted to leave Iowa permanently. His asking price for the practice, including equipment, was $5,000. Forrest knew that the equipment alone was easily worth that, but his total fortune was $78.00. Holding his breath, Forrest said the best he could muster up would be $1,000. McGinnis finally agreed to the amount and Forrest told him he'd have the money the next day.

Then Forrest called on the First National bank in Rockwell City. The bank manager listened politely while Forrest explained that he wanted to buy McGinnis' practice. The manager drew the forms from his desk drawer and shoved them towards the young graduate. "Of course," he said, "you're prepared to provide collateral."

Now it was Forrest's turn to pause, which he did, never taking his eyes off those of the banker. At last, he said, tapping his head, "I have the collateral right up here." Whether it was his sense of total conviction, or whether it was his audacious self-confidence, the manager agreed to lend him the money without collateral.

In his practice, Forrest was able to observe that those patients who had been fed diets rich in certain freshly grown vegetables, seemed to fare better than others. He had, in previous laboratory experiments, noted that mice, rats, rabbits and guinea pigs, given large quantities of minerals extracted from various legumes, showed dramatic improvements and recovered more speedily. Forrest had read with avid interest in scientific journals about the work of Casimir Funk.

Funk, born in Warsaw, had received his Ph.D. in organic chemistry at the University of Bern, where he worked on the synthesis of Stilbestrols. He later joined the Lister Institute in London. There, in research on beriberi, Funk developed a pyrimidine concentrate of rice polishings which was curative for beriberi in pigeons. In 1912, Funk proposed the term "vitamine" (vital amine) for organic compounds responsible in trace amounts for the cure or prevention of beriberi, scurvy, rickets and pellagra. It was at this point that Forrest realized, if by some process he could stabilize the minerals extracted from the vegetables that he was using, he might be able to effect a dynamic prophylactic as well as a therapeutic product equal to the "vitamines." Using many different techniques of processing, he arrived at one, whereby the mineral values were not diminished. Forrest has frequently said that he did not make food supplements; Nature made them. He merely put together in a special way what Nature had provided. Forrest called this product vitalized minerals, and they were used in tablet form throughout his practice.

Although much publicity in scientific circles was given to Casimir Funk's discovery, CURRENT BIOGRAPHY 1945 makes this point: "This history of the discovery of the vitamin is like that of almost every scientific discovery. An army of other workers had done research in the field before Casimir Funk made public his findings. Each had profited from the experience of those who had come before him (and) had carried the study a little further."

In spite of this premise and the fact that Forrest had developed the vitalized minerals at approximately the same time as Funk's "vitamine" discovery, Forrest makes no claims to originality. Says Forrest, "Every thought that has ever been produced by man, or ever will be produced, is here on this earth now. We are blanketed by thoughts."

Certainly his friend, Elbert Hubbard, concurred on that score. It is possible that he conveyed those sentiments to Forrest. When asked the reason for the phenomenal success of A MESSAGE TO GARCIA, Hubbard's reply was, "There is no such thing as an original idea. It is simply an idea whose time had come."

Forrest had written to Casimir Funk in England, and now that the Polish biochemist was in the States, they corresponded, exchanging notes. Much of Funk's later work was in developing commercial pharmaceutical products.

In mid-December, 1915, Forrest and Ruth were married at the parsonage of the Christian Church. Ruth's parents had planned a reception for the newlyweds in their home. The couple entered the house by the front door and Forrest, sizing up the crowd of family and friends, got an inspiration. Propelling his bride by the arm, he hurried her through the kitchen out the back door, and like Lupino Lane, in a Vitaphone comedy, bride and groom raced to their festooned wedding car and escaped on their honeymoon.

At the time of the newlyweds arrival, Rockwell City had a population of about 2,000. The original school house which had been converted into an Opera House was now the Baptist Church. Rather grandly, the Chamber of Commerce referred to Rockwell City as "Queen of the Prairies, Golden Buckle on the Cornbelt". But, compared to the bustling city of Davenport with its population of 50,000 Rockwell City was a rural, almost sleepy town.

The young bride got an inkling of how hard her husband would have to work as soon as they got off the train. Waiting for them at the depot was a farmer whose wife needed care. Snow and sleet had made the roads impassable for cars. With no time to settle Ruth in their new house, Forrest bundled her into his horse and buggy, and made the hazardous journey to visit his patient.

Chapter XIII

IN APRIL, 1917 the United States declared war on Germany. The clinic in Rockwell City was thriving, but Forrest knew that he had outgrown it. The time had come to expand. Forrest also felt the need to respond to the summons for medical men and trained technicians. The army enlistment office was enthusiastic about his qualifications. They spoke in terms of an officer's commission, possibly the rank of major. X-ray specialists were difficult to find.

Forrest made his decision. He sold the clinic and went with Ruth, who was pregnant, to Davenport to await the review board's decision.

When it came, it was a shattering disappointment. The medical review board, consisting of general practitioners or internists, had denied the commission. Admittedly, they were eager for specialists with Forrest's experience, but they were only prepared to offer a non-commissioned rank to a chiropractor. Incensed, Forrest asked for an appointment with the board. He offered to take any tests given to allopaths for X-ray diagnosis, but the board declined to reconsider. Disappointed at this narrow approach, he decided to reestablish his clinic and contribute what he could for the welfare of a public who would value his services based on his ability, rather than on a medical category.

On the eleventh of November, Ruth gave birth to their first son. He was named Forrest Clell Shaklee, Jr. Early in 1918, Dr. Shaklee opened his offices and a sanitorium in Fort Dodge, some thirty miles from Rockwell City.

In spite of B.J. Palmer's purist approach to Chiropractic, it was time, Forrest thought, to incorporate *all the specialities of medicine.* The offices in the now defunct Wahkonsa Hotel boasted thirty-two treating rooms and a staff of chiropractors, osteopaths, internists, general practitioners, and surgeons. In addition to his role in intricate X-ray diagnosis, Forrest was Administrator. The fifteen-bed sanitorium was located on a corner of 16th Street and Fifth Avenue. It was here that Forrest could maintain patients on diets that were rich in vitamins, and where he could assess their needs for diet supplements, such as calcium, alfalfa, and iron. In a modest way, the Shaklee clinic emulated the central medical services, so successfully operated by the Mayo brothers in Rochester, Minnesota, and was the forerunner of such membership organizations as the Permanente Hospitals of the Kaiser Foundation in California. Fort Dodge, with its population of some 20,000, swarmed to the offices in the Wahkonsa complex. At age twenty-four, Forrest was on his way to becoming a wealthy man.

The war ended that year and armistice day fell on Forrest, Jr's. first birthday. The success of his clinic caused Forrest's bankers to urge him to diversify his profits. Forrest has always maintained that he is not a businessman, but heeding his banker's advice, Forrest examined several avenues of investment. Most of them provided none of the color that he sought in work. A Scandinavian by the name of Andersen came to him with a proposal that seemed less run-of-the-mill, and which engaged his interest. In those days film rights were sold to states. Andersen felt, as it turned out accurately, that there was much money to be made in various aspects of film distribution and theater renovation. A company called Forrest Enterprises was established which would obtain distribution of films for the states of Iowa and Nebraska and would, as well, provide such theater accoutrements as folding seats, playbills, programs and advertisements.

Forrest Enterprises secured the rights for the Iowa-Nebraska distribution of D.W. Griffith's masterpiece, "Intolerance." A brash young salesman, William Rosenberg, who was called Billy, was hired to get theater bookings for the film. It was also Billy's job to secure advertising from local

129

dealers to be painted on the heavy screen that came down behind the curtain. In addition, Billy was to take orders for the collateral supplies connected with theater promotion and refurbishing. Fast talking and a whiz at taking dictation, (he had already won several prizes for his skill at shorthand) Billy appeared to be a very promising member of Forrest Enterprises.

Dr. Shaklee tells of two interesting sidelights on the film industry of those days, both of which concern "Intolerance." Having been introduced some years earlier, it had presumably gone through its road show cycle by the late teens. Portions of the film, starring Bessie Love, were cut out of it and spliced together to make a separate feature film titled, "Mother and the Law." Theater owners in the Iowa-Nebraska circuit could take their pick of either or both films. Forrest remembers Bessie Love as a winsome young girl, unspoiled as yet by the star system that was beginning to develop in Hollywood. Forrest and Ruth had developed a close friendship with her and her uncle.

The other anecdote relates to a time when Dr. Shaklee came upon his managers reviewing a copy of "Intolerance" to see if it could hold up to additional screenings. In the middle of the Egyptian pageant, replete with camel drivers and slave girls casting rose petals, Dr. Shaklee asked the projectionist to reverse the scene and at a certain point told him to "freeze" the frame. In the right hand corner at the top of the screen were both front wheels with a crank sticking out and the windshield of a Model T Ford. The tell-tale frames were, of course, cut out of the film, but Forrest wondered how many prints all over the country had shown the famous Egyptian scene intact with the Model T Ford.

Forrest Enterprises did very well except for the fact that eager young Billy contracted for supplies far above demand, and cost the company a great deal of money in excess inventory. Because of this and other high-flown schemes, Doctor Shaklee was obliged to let Billy go. One of Billy's proposals before leaving was to stage hometown movies depicting Western-style mock shoot-outs, or horse races. These would be sponsored by local merchants whose business would be featured either as background or serve as the locale for the film. Ruefully, Dr. Shaklee concedes that the novelty of the idea in those early days of film might have made him enormously wealthy, but by then he had enough of Billy's get-rich-quick propositions. Dr. Shaklee did not see Billy again until 1939. It was at the San Francisco World's Fair and the now famous Billy Rose invited him to be a guest at his Acquacade.

The year 1919 was an auspicious one for Forrest, blighted only by one sad incident. Late in March, Forrest took time off from his flourishing practice in Fort Dodge to visit his family. Ralph and Cecily were now both married, and most of all, Forrest wanted his grandfather David Overton to see his first-born, Forrest, Jr.

The family, including David's children, Martha Shaklee, Eli Overton and his wife Edith, and his three other sons, their wives and children, gathered at the patriarch's home in South Carlisle. David, nearing eighty-three, looked robust and was as usual in fine spirits. The ambience of his twenty grandchildren and seventeen great-grandchildren, never failed to bring joviality to him, while to them he must have seemed an eternal Saint Nicholas.

After the noon meal had been served and cleared, David took his family through a customary tour of his prized orchards. At some point, one of the family noticed that David was no longer shepherding the group. A quick search revealed him lying in an arbor where he had collapsed. It was at first thought that he had died, but he lived on for a week. In its obituary, the *Indianola Herald* said that he had died of paralepsis. But, Forrest, remembering the scout and rifleman legend of his maternal grandfather, preferred to think that David had passed away that afternoon in the full pride of showing his beloved orchards.

The success of Forrest's clinic was such that he was receiving more and more requests for house-calls from rural areas. In order to reach patients within a 100-mile radius, he purchased a two-passenger Curtiss plane from Anderson & Dart of the Fort Dodge Airplane Company, thereby becoming if not the first doctor in the United States to make housecalls by plane, at least the first flying doctor in Iowa. He is quoted in a headline article of the *Fort Dodge Messenger and Chronicle* (July 29, 1919) as saying that he had not been able to accept many out-of-town calls because of the delay in making railroad connections and also due to the uncertainty of the roads in autoing. "With the plane," said Dr. Shaklee, "I can be there almost before the patient has time to hang up the receiver!" The *Messenger* article concluded with:

> "—But—*voila*—the airplane crosses out all of these objections. Of course, rain does interfere with air driving, but in weather we are having what a snap it would be.
>
> Grandmothers have been pictured for lo these many years when modern inventions come on apace as raising their eyes to heaven, and wondering 'what are we coming to?' Now the question is 'where are we at?'
>
> Who will be the next one to use an airplane? Will it be the grocer, the milkman, the iceman or merely the real estate dealer?"

The demand for the doctor in the flying machine became increasingly great. Forrest found that people were using any pretext to have him make one of his airplane calls. He also discovered that merchants in neighboring towns were not above capitalizing on his visits. Responding to an emergency call, he would sometimes find that the fields which served as landing grounds would be crowded with sightseers and lined on both sides with youths carrying placards advertising local businesses. To temper this type of exploitation and, if for nothing else but to ease the strain of making the virtually

132

unnecessary trips, Forrest was obliged to charge $100 per "plane call" as he puts it.

Forrest and his plane had also created quite a stir in international chiropractic circles. B.J. Palmer had said, "Early to bed and early to rise, work like hell and advertise." And, here was one of his former students who was doing it and doing it within the ethical context of making house calls.

B.J., maintaining his purist chiropractic attitude, expressed disdain for Forrest's wide-spectrum approach to the treatment of *dis*-ease. He referred to Forrest's venture as "Shaklee's pseudo-clinics." "One service does *not* do it all," Forrest insisted and the overwhelming success of his total service medical clinics were proof of it. B.J. was miffed at the inventiveness of his one-time pupil.

The 5th annual Lyceum and the 14th annual Chiropractors Convention was to be held in Davenport. Scheduled for August, the event was widely publicized. Attending were representatives of 26 foreign countries. Thirteen New Zealand Chiropractors had travelled 8,000 miles to attend the meetings. But, what commanded the most attention both in the press and at the convention itself, was the journey made by Forrest from Fort Dodge to Davenport. In its August 4th issue, the *Fort Dodge Messenger and Chronicle* outlined plans for the flight with the heading DAVENPORT WILL WELCOME SHAKLEE.

> "Dr. F.C. Shaklee, local chiropractor, will receive an official welcome from the city of Davenport when he reaches that place by airplane Sunday, August 23, the first day of the chiropractic convention. Dr. Shaklee will arrive at Davenport at 10 a.m. and will be officially received at the Davenport mile track, which is located northwest of the city.
>
> Dr. Shaklee will fly over the Rock Island depot upon the arrival of the chiropractic special from Chicago, and over the line of march during the parade Wednesday."

On Sunday, August 24th, the *Davenport Democrat* heralded the first day of the convention, and went on to say that over 3,000 chiropractors had already registered. The article described how they had arrived by every mode of travel thinkable, including an airplane flown by Dr. Shaklee of Fort Dodge. "This distance of 368 miles took him a trifle over three and a half hours in his Curtiss machine. An interesting feature in connection with Dr. Shaklee's flight here will be the christening of the airplane. The plane will be christened "B.J." as a courtesy to Dr. B.J. Palmer, head of the Palmer School of Chiropactors."

Mollified by Forrest's graceful gesture, B.J. had accepted the compliment and the christening was a convention highlight. Gathered in West Davenport, at the Locomotive Works Grounds where the plane was anchored, were thousands of curious spectators. The *Davenport Democrat* described the actual christening in these words, ". . .when the time came a bottle of sparkling liquid was produced which looked like the real thing. At any rate when the bottle was broken over the prow of the machine, in the good old fashioned way, a howl went up from the bystanders, caused no doubt by their realization and regret at the waste. . ." Actually the howl was probably the loudest from Ruth and Mabel Palmer who were drenched to the skin from the contents of the smashed bottle.

The city of Davenport had cooperated to the fullest extent with gaily festooned streets, tours, band playing, motorcades, and speeches by top officials, led by Mayor Lee J. Dougherty. A monster parade was slated for the following Wednesday. This was to feature floats which had been worked on by over 200 artisans. A spine, 50 feet long and carried by a score of men and boys, was to occupy a prominent place in the line of march. Overhead, Dr. Shaklee would fly, scattering leaflets on which were printed the Chiropractic motto, "Keep smiling." This feature of the parade was described by a local paper as Dr. Shaklee's shower of smiles. Recalling the incident, Forrest says that the shower of smiles almost turned into a curtain of tragedy. The crowds were gathered and milling around, anxious for the airplane demonstration to begin. As Forrest hove into view, a deafening cheer went up. Forrest circled the street scattering leaflets and prepared to land as he swooped downwards, grandstanding for the excitement of the crowd. He suddenly found that the control strick was jammed and that he could not bring it up. The throngs of people assembled below became more distinct. He was approaching them at what seemed a furious speed. Still the stick would not budge. Now he could see faces as he desperately pulled back at the stick—an unearthly silence engulfed him as if the thousands of onlookers had caught one gigantic breath. As it seemed certain that he would crash into the street, the stick eased and he pulled it back with all his might, seeming just to clear the heads of the people below. When he brought the plane down on a nearby field, Forrest realized that the audience had interpreted the close call as a brilliantly executed stunt.

Chapter XIV

BY THE following year, the reputation of the Shaklee clinic was such that Forrest could intensify his research on diet supplementation and concentrate on X-ray diagnosis. Not too much was known about the workings or possible long-range side-effects of this medium, but it was acknowledged as a valuable diagnostic tool, particularly for the visualization of bones. The immediate hazards of radiation were known to all X-ray technicians. To prevent electromagnetic radiation, certain precautions were taken. Lead impregnated rubber aprons and gloves, which were thought to be adequate protection, were worn to protect the torso and hands of the radiologists. In simple terms, Dr. Shaklee describes how those early systems worked.

"You're standing in front of the fluoroscope, looking. The rays are shooting directly at the screen, coming through the body of the patient and giving us an image on the screen. There is a little target in the center of the X-ray tube. The target is at a 45 degree angle with its point at the center. The rays strike the target and branch straight down onto the patient and through him, taking the picture. What we didn't realize is that these rays were scattering out from the target. They'd hit a metal pipe on the wall, for example, and bounce back on the technician." The ionizing radiation resulted in burns on Dr. Shaklee's left shoulder and left hip, which began to ulcerate. The brother of an osteopath who worked at the clinic was a leading cancer specialist in Chicago. At the osteopath's urging, Forrest went to Chicago. There the cancer specialist's prognosis was grim. The arm would have to be amputated at the shoulder.

"And what about my hip?" Forrest asked.

"You will have to lose your leg up to the hip", said the specialist, adding that the amputations would probably

136

arrest the spreading of the carcinoma for a few months.

"In that case, I think I'll die in one piece," said Forrest Shaklee. At the cancer specialist's advice, Forrest journeyed to the Mayo Clinic in Minnesota. Here the prognosis was no better. The process of treating cancer with radiation therapy was not yet in practice and the proposal again was to amputate. Forrest reiterated his intention of remaining whole.

On the train back to Iowa, Forrest's mask of bravado dropped. He was, after all, a very young man. He had one young son and his wife was expecting again. The future had looked so promising and now he was being offered the option of dismemberment, and only as a stay of execution. Both the doctor in Chicago and the Mayo Clinic were positive that the cancer would become progressive—he would die.

It was then that Forrest made his decision—he would *not* die. If there was anything to his theories that healthy cells could be built by proper nutrition, now was the time to prove it. And, he would prove it on himself. Over and over again in his clinics he had seen results that were miraculous. How much of it was faith? Why then, he would have faith in what diet could effect in the regeneration of the body. Listening to the rattle of the train wheels, Forrest seemed to hear, "What you think, you look; what you think, you do; What you think, you are." "Well," Forrest said in response to the wheels, "I *think* I'm going to live!"

By the time Forrest returned home, his resolve was firm and he looked optimistically towards a future. Within weeks, the offices and clinic were sold and Forrest and his family moved back to Davenport. Now began an intensive regimen of nutrition, continual blood analysis and occasional fasting. To ensure that what he consumed was the freshest, Forrest would drive out to the farmers and buy the vegetables and fruit almost as they were spaded up from the soil. For weeks and even months, there were no visible changes in the ulcerated sores on shoulder and hip, and the pain was almost unbearable. But, Forrest lost neither courage nor belief in the final outcome. He supplemented his all-fresh diet with

137

vitamins and minerals, ingesting amounts that were, for those days, considered megadoses.

On December 2, 1921, Ruth gave birth to another child. In his youth, Forrest had been friends with a lad named Raleigh. He had always liked both the boy and the name, so he called his second son Raleigh.

Within a year, the sores had stopped festering. By the end of 1922, the sores on his shoulder and hip had healed over completely with healthy tissue. He had renewed energy, and with it a sense of vindication, not only over life itself, but for what he was doing in nutrition, and for what he knew now, beyond any doubt, that he could do for others. At his annual checkup in the Chicago clinic, the specialist listened tolerantly as Forrest described his program. He shook his head disbelievingly and replied, "It was a remission, pure and simple. Healthy cells had overcome the cancerous cells and that was the cause of the remission, but there could be no guarantee of a permanent cure." Likewise, at the Mayo Clinic; beyond acknowledging that a full and remarkable remission had been effected, no one seemed to want to pursue *why* the cells had become healthy enough to overcome the carcinogenic cells and tissue. The medical word was remission; in another time that word might have been miracle.

Forrest realized that there were many factors involved in his cure; to begin with, he had had the advantage of a basically healthy body. But, he had also allowed Nature to heal and mend him in Her way and using Her means. He was careful to point out then, and reminds us now, that there is no standard dietary regimen for treating *dis*-ease. What is enough for one system, may not be nearly enough for another. Conversely, what is adequate for one, may be far too much for another. Balance, testing and judicious experiment on a subjective level were all vitally important guidelines to therapy. For those very reasons, Forrest will not define megadoses; will not give pat dietary regimens with so much of one or more vitamins, so many minerals—or

138

such and such amounts of protein. "Nature made us individual complexes and we must approach ourselves and our needs accordingly," says he.

With the recovery of his vitality came the need to work again, but Forrest wanted to be very sure of his next move. While investigating the most lucrative area for his next clinic, he became Chief of Staff of what was then the largest drugless clinic in the world.

By the time Forrest decided to move his family to Mason City, Iowa, it was July of 1924. Forrest, Jr. was going on seven and Raleigh was nearly three.

Forrest established his offices on the main floor of the Cerro Gordo Hotel. There were the usual treatment rooms, and a spacious area devoted to X-ray equipment and storage of films. Then, as now, radiology equipment was extremely expensive. His formulations for food supplements were being packaged and dispensed to all patients with nutritional disorders.

The *Mason City Globe Gazette,* in its 75th Anniversary Edition, considered the opening of the Shaklee Clinic sufficiently important to carry the story. The lead article was titled, "Shaklee Heads Local Clinic."

> "Dr. F.C. Shaklee had had 12 years of experience in the care of the sick, both in private practice and in hospital and sanitarium work. As a young man he was graduated from the Palmer School of Chiropractic. He had previously studied under Dr. Ernest Thompson carrying an experimental work in the X-ray laboratory. . .
>
> . . .January 1st, Dr. Shaklee resigned as head of the (Davenport) institution and came to Mason City establishing the Shaklee Clinic, which is composed of the leading chiropractors of Northern Iowa. The purpose of this organization is to improve the service of each member. When asked what he believed to be the greatest aid in restoring health to the pa-

139

tient, Dr. Shaklee replied, 'common sense, the most uncommon thing in the world.' "

Perhaps as Forrest made the statement he was remembering the robber in the woods in Davenport who refused to believe he didn't have a nickel.

The person most proud of Forrest's success was his father, Robert. Now, he and his son could jokingly recall the time, almost ten years before, when Forrest had applied for his loan to buy McGinnis' practice. They remembered Martha's trepidation at the sum. A thousand dollars had seemed such a huge amount to have to repay. Robert's pride was enhanced by the knowledge that his son had made it on his own. On occasions when Robert had suspected that Forrest was in need and had mailed him checks, Forrest had always returned them with a polite note of thanks.

For his part, Forrest took much pleasure in the visits from his father and, since Robert had been retired for a couple of years, these were more frequent.

One day, Robert had some business to attend to in Bevington, five miles below Patterson. Later, Robert was waiting on the Bevington Platform for the freight train back to Patterson. The section men were through with their shift and seeing Robert, hailed him. Robert was immensely well liked and known as "Dad," to the railroad workers whose section ran from Bevington to Winterset. The men who were returning to Patterson offered Robert a ride in their tool car. The tool car, stacked with picks, shovels and gear in racks, was attached to the handcar, which consisted, in the main, of a platform on wheels and was operated by either a pump or by motor. Robert was seated on the tool box built across the front of the car. The workers got on to the handcar, operating it by gas. The two cars rollicked along at a fairly high speed with no mishap, until they came to a curve around the hill alongside of the river. The handcar negotiated the curb, but the acceleration caused the tool car to jump the tracks. Robert was thrown on to the ties, and as he lay there stunned, the tool car came barreling down on top of him. Beyond a few cuts and bruises, Robert suffered little external damage, but he was unconscious.

Upon being notified, Forrest went to his side immediately. For some time, Robert remained unconscious and Forrest stayed with him. Even in his comatose state, Robert seemed aware of his favorite son's presence. If Forrest patted his knee or held his hand, Robert rested gently. The nurses reported that when Forrest left the room, the patient became restless. Three weeks later, Robert was discharged from the hospital and claimed to be feeling fine. But, as soon as Robert was able to make the trip to Mason City, Forrest put him in his clinic, where Robert underwent extensive X-rays and a series of tests. Robert had had a skull fracture, but it seemed to be mending satisfactorily.

By autumn, Forrest and Robert went pheasant hunting and Robert seemed fully recovered. Over the next year, he occasionally mentioned that all was not well with him; that he suffered sharp shooting pains in his head. This he did diffidently, as a man accustomed to being stalwart. Forrest did not disregard the hesitantly offered complaints. Again and then again, Robert was put through X-ray and blood tests, and always they revealed nothing.

In July of 1925, when it seemed that Robert was beyond any danger and Forrest was, once more steeped in his own work, death claimed another old friend, William Jennings Bryan.

Dayton, Tennessee had become the focal point of a case that engrossed America. The Scopes trial was headlined across the newspapers of the country. The chief protagonists were Clarence Darrow, for the defense, William Jennings Bryan, the prosecuting attorney, and almost least important, a young school teacher named John T. Scopes, who had defied the Tennessee law that forbade teaching evolution in school. While schools in Tennessee accepted the scientific fact that the earth is round and not flat, that day and night were caused by the revolution of the earth on its axis, the

Darwinian Theory, that man, as all creatures, evolved from the sea, was forbidden by law in the states of Tennessee and Mississippi.

Spearheading the movement to control teachers from spreading knowledge of evolution, was a group called the Fundamentalists. This group held that everything written in the old and new Testaments was literally true. Any contradictions, however scientifically based, was considered heresy. Bryan, naturally, fell into the role of leader and as such, he was invited to prosecute Scopes. Darrow leaped at the chance to defend the school teacher, mainly as a means of drawing national attention to what he considered to be the case against science.

Because of what Scopes had done, he was found guilty and fined the maximum of $100. The case was appealed and the Supreme Court later reversed and dismissed it. But, at the trial, Darrow managed, through his scalpel sharp dissection of Bryan's orthodoxy, to make Bryan contradict himself and ultimately, to look absurd.

Bryan died almost immediately after the trial. In his book, MY LIFE, Darrow mentions the fact that Bryan ate a big meal and attributes his death to a combination of overeating, the Tennessee heat and anxieties over the trial. He points out ironically, that the greatest proponent for prohibition died of overeating.

In point of fact, Bryan ate nothing on that hot summer's day when he went to his room to rest. He never woke up.

Biographers have tended to treat Bryan rather harshly, emphasizing the extremes of his brilliant oratory and the narrowness of his education and intellect. But, Forrest remembered more than the shining presence and beguiling voice. He recalls the unaffected warmth of the man who truly felt that he was the Great Commoner. Forrest points out that while Bryan later opposed it, what became the League of Nations was originally his inspiration. And, while his fervor for Prohibition was unbridled, he was, equally, a champion for women's suffrage. That he was violently antiwar might have made him a hero in this day and age, although in his, it only served to compound his political unpopularity. Ultimately, however, he had millions of admirers and they were the people whom he had addressed for over a quarter of a century. Forrest remained among these.

Robert Shaklee died the following spring at the age of fifty-nine.

On a fine March morning, Robert was in the kitchen sitting in his rocker, and reading "Wallace's Farmer." Martha was preparing the noon meal. She planned to serve parsnips as the vegetable course, and had earlier dug them out of the earth where they had been left all winter. Martha was assembling her cooking ingredients in the closed-in porch, which served as additional work space for the kitchen. When Robert saw the slim crop of parsnips, he said jokingly, "Better not drop any of these, they'll go through the slats in the floor." It was the last thing he ever said. As Martha set the food on the kitchen table, she called to her husband. When there was no reply, she glanced at him and then went up to him and tilted his chin with her hand. The copy of "Wallace's Farmer" fell to the floor as his head lolled back lifelessly.

Forrest's shock at his father's death was compounded by grief. And, with the grief came self-doubt and recrimination. Robert had maintained, as recently as his last examination, that there was something wrong with his head. But, the X-ray plates revealed nothing other than the skull fracture which had seemed to be healing. There was no evidence in the plates of a tumor or any other type of growth. The highly sensitive film used today for X-ray diagnosis was as yet unknown. Although he was successful professionally, content in his marriage and a doting father, Forrest felt an incalculable loss. With the death of his father, a way of life had ended forever.

143

Chapter XV

WHAT FORREST SHAKLEE has in common with other successful men, is the work inspiration. It has never left him. While poets and writers might wait for the muse to bestir their talents, Forrest seemed to have been dictated to by an unfailing source, he calls creative energy. "Everything I have ever done has been forced upon me," says Forrest. He does not make this claim as one protesting a burden, but rather as a person who accepts being the instrument of a greater force. What is that force? Inevitably Forrest's response is simply, "Nature." Nature has guided him in all things. When projects went awry, the fault was his for not heeding Nature's counsel as it was intended. Or perhaps, Nature intended that he take those misdirected steps in order to learn from them. "Life is a never-ceasing school from which there is no graduation," Forrest maintains. "You stop learning and you're dead." It is as good a credo as any, and based on his success, has proven highly workable.

In 1927 the world was agog with the exploits of a young flyer who had made the trans-Atlantic flight from Garden City, New York, to Le Bourget, near Paris in 33½ hours. By late summer, Charles Lindbergh was on an aeroplane tour of the United States with the purpose of visiting one or more cities in each state.

The tour was sponsored by the Daniel Guggenheim fund. Its purpose was to encourage popular interest in aviation and to focus attention on air transportation, especially on the air mail.

Colonel Hanford MacNider, Acting Secretary of War, had persuaded Lindbergh to make the tour. MacNider's father was president of the First National Bank in Mason City, and the family was patients of Dr. Shaklee.

Needless to say, Mason City pulled out all the stops to welcome the hero of the skies, and the newspapers fairly burbled with accounts of the unassuming young pilot and his famous smile. Lindbergh was perhaps the last young national hero before the depression swept over the country.

Hanford MacNider, known as Jack to his friends, was to preside at the dedication of the new Legion airport west of the city. On Friday, a giant Fokker plane bearing MacNider's party arrived. The Saturday, August 27th issue of the *Mason City Globe Gazette*, carried this account:

> "A large three motored army monoplane circled about the Legion flying field once Friday afternoon, roared away to the north, and then glided easily to the ground, almost touching the telephone wires on the south side of the Clear Lake concrete highway near the Legion airport.

> "When the giant airplane had come to a stop near the new hangar which is being constructed at the field, a door in the roomy and comfortable passenger compartment opened and Col. Hanford MacNider, assistant secretary of war, Mrs. MacNider and a group of fellow passengers stepped out as they might have stepped down from the steps of a Pullman car. Col. MacNider is here for the Legion airport dedication Sunday. . .

> "An average of more than 100 miles an hour was made over some stretches of the trip on Friday. This figure seems marvelous after one has seen the plane. It does not seem possible that such a large body could be lifted from the ground except by a derrick, and it seems almost incredible that the three small propellors will carry the machine high in the air and over many miles at a high rate of speed.

> "The army plane in which Col. MacNider came here is similar to ones used by Commander Byrd on his

145

trans-Atlantic flight and Liut. Maitland on his trans-Pacific flight. Maitland has been using the plane since his return to the United States, and he left it at the Ohio field for the MacNider party on Friday.

"No stop was made for lunch. Provisions had been made for a light meal and the passengers dined aboard the plane.

"The Fokker plane used by the MacNider party attracted hundreds of interested persons Friday night and today. A guard was on duty thruout the night and today the cabin of the giant bird was opened for a time one time early this afternoon. . ."

A dozen planes from Selfridge field were to be flown as a pursuit squadron on Sunday. The pilots who arrived on Saturday were entertained along with Lindbergh, at MacNider's Clear Lake estates, five miles west of Mason City.

Among the guests at the dinner dance in Clear Lake were Forrest and his wife. Because of his long standing interest in flying and his personal friendship with the MacNider family, Forrest was invited to stay over in a guest cottage on the estate.

MacNider was a speedboat enthusiast and at daybreak, he roused Forrest with the purpose of taking him and the young aviator for a spin on Clear Lake. MacNider's boat was called the "Betsy Ross," and it was plainly his pride and joy. But, he invited Lindbergh to pilot the boat, and, as Forrest remembers, "We went up and down that 3 ½ mile lake in no time flat." He admits with a chuckle, "there were several moments when I had a lump in my throat as I hung on to the gunwhales watching the boats tied to the dock, which we seemed to be heading directly into. But Lindy was a marvelous man in a boat as well as in the air, and in spite of my fears, there was no accident."

The Selfridge Flyers were to perform on Sunday at the

official dedication of the airport. Whether or not Lindbergh would join the pursuit squadron remained a mystery. The public was keyed to great expectancy. Lindbergh had earlier said to MacNider that he had seen the Selfridge Flyers perform on his visit to Detroit and, that in his opinion, they were the best flyers he had ever seen and that they excelled by far anything of their kind in Europe.

"I'll go 800 miles anytime to see those boys perform," he told the Acting Secretary of War. This, in effect, was why MacNider had suggested to Lindbergh that, by hopping 200 miles off his scheduled itinerary, he could once again see the famous Selfridge Squadron in operation.

Until Lindbergh had actually arrived, the army officials gave no assurance that he would join the squadron in their program. The *Mason City Globe Gazette* reported:

> "Commander Kew repeated his former assertion that those in charge were making no promises of Lindbergh at the dedication and made it clear that there was no assurance that in the event of his being there that everybody would be able to see him.
>
> "He will be in this locality in a purely unofficial way and his contract with the Guggenheim foundation is of such character that it would be a violation of one of its provisions to assume a part in our program," said Mr. Kew. "His status at the affair will be that of any other person who gains admission.
>
> "If he chooses to fly one of the pursuit planes, or present himself to the crowd, we naturally would be glad to have him do so. But we're giving no pledges. It will be the biggest air event Iowa has ever seen, regardless of whether Lindbergh is there. The program will stand on its own feet."

And, MacNider is quoted as adding:

147

"The pursuit squadron will perform all its formations as a unit, according to Mr. MacNider. There is no such thing as a solo performance. Nothing in the field of aviation, probably, is more spectacular than a pursuit squadron's activities, flying extremely close together at times. During the time that the squadron is in action, the blimps will be cruising over the field."

But, Lindbergh had shown. And, on that Sunday afternoon, although the weather had been forecast as cloudy, it was fairly clear and over 25,000 people crammed the airport and surrounding areas for a glimpse of the national hero. Among the spectators were Forrest, his wife, and their two sons.

Both Forrest, Jr. and Raleigh remember the event. Forrest, Jr. recalls that the dedication was responsible for the largest gathering of aircraft in the history of Iowa. In addition to the Selfridge Squadron of 12 planes, were the RS-1 blimp from Scott Field, Illinois and the monster Fokker plane that had transported the Acting Secretary of War. Lindbergh was to fly the "Spirit of Unrest," which he flew in from Sioux City.

"Quite an airshow for those pre-commercial aviation days," muses Forrest, Jr.

Raleigh remembers the overwhelming ovation given to the air hero, cries of, "Here comes Lindy," taken up in a chorus of, "Lindy, Lindy, Lindy!" which became deafening. He remembers the aviator's warm quick smile to the crowd and a wave of his hand.

The air maneuvers took place in the afternoon following the airport dedication ceremony. Patiently the crowds had waited for the excitement of the pursuit squadron to begin. The twelve planes were parked along the front of the port with space between them and the fence for fueling. The *Globe-Gazette* described the scene:

"Col. Lindbergh himself, walked down to the big
Fokker plane where the parachutes were stored and
got his own chute permitting thousands of others
along the crowded sidelines to get a glimpse of
him.

"Major Lanphier gave his orders.

"We fly up in elements and land individually in the
Luffbery circle," he said. "Slim, Lieut Woodring and
I will form the first elements. Are we all here?"

"I think we are sir," said one of the pilots.

"The youthful hero flew off Major Lanphier's right
wing in the first of the four v-shaped elements in
the squadron, each V being composed of three
planes."

The *Globe Gazette* went on to describe the planes, which
were the most rapid aircraft in existence, capable of doing
200 miles an hour. The small biplanes with 230 horsepower
engines were exceptionally maneuverable.

". . .The manner in which Col. Lindbergh and his
associates handles them in battle formations, curves
and dives and finally ending up with the Luffbery
circle represented the highest development in flying
and kept the immense throng thrilled for half an
hour."

"The 12 planes went up three at a time in rapid
succession. After the last trio had joined their
comrades, Major Lanphier began to give commands
for various formations, which were carried out in a
manner that showed almost uncanny ability to
handle the planes. The planes flew within 20 feet of
each other in each element and executed difficult
movements and dives that kept the throng marveling."

Lindbergh left Mason City the following morning and

was driven to the airport by MacNider. Monday's *Globe Gazette,* in its lead article expressed their views of the young hero:

> "The lone eagle of the Atlantic, who had dined with kings, hobnobbed with the rich and powerful in dazzling settings, been overwhelmed by the ovations of millions on two continents and who was selected as the one figure in America to carry out the program of the Guggenheim foundation for the promotion of aviation, dropped back Sunday to the rank of cadet flyer on the local field and placed himself under the command of Major T.G. Lanphier, who was in charge of the brilliant squadron from Michigan. . ."

> "Col. Lindbergh's part with the brilliant pursuit squadron from Michigan was, of course, the feature of the day—that and the famous Lindbergh smile which won the admiring multitude wherever the famous aviator was in sight."

What did not appear in any news account was the personally guided tour over Mason City on which Lindbergh took Forrest. Learning from MacNider that Forrest had flown his own plane since 1919, he invited Forrest to join him for a spin in the "Spirit of Unrest." Forrest accepted the invitation and drove the aviator out to the airport early one morning, before the crowds had arrived. He still recalls the thrill of flying with Lindbergh in that 10-minute jaunt over the city, "Lindy's skill was breathtaking." Lindbergh offered Forrest the controls, which he says, "I had the good sense to decline. I was nowhere the pilot he was and if anything had gone wrong, what a blot on my conscience"—and adds with typical Forrest Shaklee wit, "to say nothing of my life—"

Although Forrest saw Lindbergh on several other public occasions, they never again met on a personal level.

Part IV

AND HIS WORK

Chapter XVI

FOR THE year following Lindbergh's visit, Forrest busied himself, extending his clinics to outlying areas. Dr. Ralph Ulrich of Garner, Iowa remembers that Forrest would go to neighboring towns and help conduct free clinics. Because of his reputation, Forrest would lend his name to these clinics. Says Dr. Ulrich, "In those days we were having tough times just to keep on our feet. Three or four of us doctors would meet and devote an evening, or a full day, examining patients. This is the way we built our business. Forrest was always organizing us and he wasn't making anything out of it himself. But in a way, I guess that was helping him too. He was getting a lot of publicity. And—even in those days he was far ahead of most doctors as far as food is concerned—nutrition. . ."

Floy Moretz Dahl, of Manly, Iowa remembers that her father "doctored" with Forrest. "Doctoring" was a colloquial term used for being treated. She submits a patient case history chart from Dr. Shaklee's clinic in the Cerro Gordo Hotel dated January, 1928. On the chart, Forrest has checked the foods that Mr. Moretz could eat and those which should be avoided. Bread was designated as whole wheat, egg yolks are restricted, while egg whites are permissible. The recommended diet on the back page, suggests a wide variety of vegetables, fish, white meat of chicken, no sugar and no fats. In addition, Mr. Moretz was no doubt given vitalized minerals.

In spite of his busy schedule, Forrest made time for his young sons. Both Forrest, Jr. and Raleigh remember helping in their father's lab. The help consisted mainly of filling capsules and putting them into bottles.

Raleigh recalls that the formulas were in powdered form, "my brother and I, as children, would sit there filling gelatin capsules by hand—tamp-tamp-tamp."

Remembering his own childhood, Forrest encouraged their interest in music. Forrest, Jr. played the trumpet and Lee, the baritone in the school band.

Forrest had, for some time, been cooperating with the minister of the Christian Church in Mason City. Aided by a file of sermons inherited from his grandfather, David Shaklee, Forrest made a commanding presence. He had a fine resonant voice and his sermons were widely attended. As a result, he was invited by the elders of the church in Portland, Iowa to fill in, while they attempted to find a full-time minister. This went on for several months, with Forrest giving up his Sundays, while the church interviewed various candidates. Finally, the elders called a meeting to vote on who among the candidates would be best suited. Forrest was startled to hear that he had been chosen unanimously. This presented a problem.

To officiate on a regular basis, he must be an ordained minister. While Forrest had completed his study and received his degree of Doctor of Divinity, he had not been ordained by the church. But, on January 6, 1929, the elders of the Church of Christ in Mason City, Iowa, endorsed by the other churches in the city, ordained him as a minister.

It was part of the rounding of Forrest's character that he enjoyed the church meetings, enjoyed theological argument and enjoyed presenting sermons. It was the reverse side of his scientist's nature. But, his technical side was equally occupied with his interest in inventions.

One of his earliest interests was the new phonograph, or

vitaphone as it was called. Bothered by the distortions on phonograph cylinders, Forrest had reasoned that if he could pick up the vibrations in the dead center and transfer them to a disc, he could control the static. After numerous experiments, he had sent off the designs to a patent attorney in Washington D.C. Months later, he received a reply informing him that the patent for such an invention had already been filed by Thomas Edison.

In the nineteen twenties, Edison, Henry Ford and Harvey Firestone were involved in chemurgy, the industrial use of agricultural products. Ford experimented with plastics and fiber made from soybean—and extended to lettuce, sugar cane, and sweet potatoes. Since rubber was supplied by the laticiferous trees of the tropics, American experiments had been limited to plants such as Milkweed, Dogbanes and Spurges. Edison was said to be trying to find and develop a latex-bearing plant that could be grown anywhere in the states, and that would yield a superior quality of rubber. To that end, and with his characteristic thoroughness, Edison determined to cut and test all plants in the United States.

Because Forrest did not believe that rubber derived from domestic natural sources was practical, he had been working on a rubber-like compound, made entirely of synthetics. The formula was developed in the secrecy of his labs, and when one of the composites appeared to have all, or most, of the characteristics of natural rubber, Forrest ordered tire molds to his specifications. From the molds he produced tires that were used not only on his personal car, but on the clinic truck as well. The synthetic rubber proved durable over months of testing. In late 1928, Forrest attempted to patent his invention, this time choosing an eminent patent attorney in Chicago. He was informed that the search would take time. Busy with his clinic work, Forrest thought no more about the matter.

In January of 1929, what he remembers as the coldest night of his recollection, Dr. Shaklee received a phone call telling him that the Cerro Gordo Hotel was on fire. Upon

153

arriving at the scene, it seemed to him that flames had spread to the second floor. Smoke was billowing from beneath the roof of the porch in front of the building. The Cecil theater, adjacent to the hotel, was packed at the time and appeared to be threatened. In the lobby of the hotel, the guests were assembled, some in states of undress, some carrying grips into which they had thrust their valuables. Consulting with the firemen, Forrest learned that the fire's origin was unknown but that it was on the ground floor, and most likely in his office.

With the firemen, Dr. Shaklee crawled on his hands and knees to avoid being suffocated by the smoke. They crawled from the foyer of the hotel, through a long hall, finally locating the fire in a back room of Dr. Shaklee's office where the electrical equipment was kept. A short circuit in the wall of the building had started the fire. The flames were of such intensity that it was nearly impossible for the firemen to work. When the hoses were turned on, huge electrical flashes occurred, and it then became necessary to turn off all current in the building. Since the firemen were trying to abate the flames, Forrest insisted on making the perilous trek on hands and knees back through the hall to the front office, where the main switches were located. By now the entire ground floor was a blazing oven. Burned and almost overcome by the smoke inhalation, Forrest reached the switches. It took the firemen over an hour to douse the flames and when they were done, the loss was total. Insurance adjusters from Des Moines were on the scene the very next morning and they negotiated a substantial settlement.

Besides the loss of his office furniture, equipment and records, all of Dr. Shaklee's files were consumed by the flames. Among these were files containing all his correspondence, but most grievous to him were the losses of his personal documents, including letters from William Jennings Bryan, and the correspondence with Casimir Funk. Miraculously undestroyed was the personally inscribed set of

154

Elbert Hubbard's "Little Journeys." Recalling this, Forrest says, "it was as if Elbert Hubbard was telling me symbolically, "that when all else is destroyed, only the product of the mind persists." To this day, the volumes sit in his office.

"What you think, you look; What you think, you do; What you think, you are." The simple thought which had developed gradually over the years into a philosophy of Nature, that man could draw on his own Inner Consciousness, sustained Forrest now and directed him. He had become financially successful and now the semaphores of Nature seemed to point the way for him to pursue his life's work. He wanted no more patients too far advanced in their diseases for recovery. Instead, he would concentrate on the research of nutrition that would help prevent that debilitation.

But, for the moment, Forrest decided that what he needed more than anything else was a vacation. Since his graduation from Palmer, fourteen years earlier, he had worked unremittingly. The west coast of Florida was a popular vacationing area, particularly for hunters. And, since in his mind, rest was not synonymous with vacationing, Forrest prepared for the journey by developing yet another invention. This was a forerunner of the camper. On a Willy's-Knight Speed truck, Forrest built what he called a touring home. He drew the plans and directed the work on the reconstruction of the vehicle. First, the wheels were extended back three feet and an extra bearing was put in the drive shaft. Then, to test the durability of his synthetic rubber, Forrest exchanged the truck tires with the tires of his own composition. He remodeled the body of the truck next to form a house. Within the "house" he built bunks for sleeping and a closet above the windshield to store fishing rods. An ice box and a gasoline stove were rude but effective appliances. A tank on the running board under the floor of the "house" provided water through a hand pump.

While this early mobile home lacked complete toilet facilities, and the family was obliged to use campground restrooms, it was still unusual enough a sight to attract attention. On their many stops between Iowa and Florida, the family was the subject of curiosity seekers who lined the highways leading out of little towns for a glimpse of the Shaklee touring home.

Forrest decided to headquarter in Fort Myers. No sooner were he and the family ensconced in a hotel, than the phone began to ring. Bewildered, Ruth, who answered the phone, told Forrest that the newspapers wanted to interview him. Believing that interest in the touring home had prompted the press' curiosity, Forrest consented to an interview. But, it was not the touring home that concerned the reporters. They had somehow learned of the synthetic rubber and were avidly curious. Since he had wanted to insure his chances of obtaining a patent for the formula, Forrest had been meticulously discreet about his invention, but plainly the news had leaked. To the reporters peppering questions, Forrest gave politely evasive replies, but, short of lying, there was no way in which he could deny the existence of the tires on his touring home.

"Did Forrest know that at this very moment, Ford, Firestone and Edison were spending millions of dollars in experiments with attempts at converting agricultural products into an industrial material?" the reporters asked. Forrest said that he had heard of their interest in chemurgy.

"Did Dr. Shaklee's visit to Fort Myers have anything to do with these experiments?" Since the idea that an established genius like Thomas Edison might have been even remotely interested in Forrest's invention, was so far from his credulity, Forrest merely laughed. He realized, however, that in the world of patents, it is frequently the tiniest slip " 'twixt cup and the lip" that can mean success or failure. And, he cautioned Ruth to accept no more calls from the press.

Early the next morning Ruth came to him after answering the phone. Amused at her obvious consternation, Forrest said, "What's the problem? More reporters?"

"It's *him*," Ruth said, thrusting the receiver at her hus-

156

band. *Him* turned out to be Thomas Edison's secretary. Mr. Edison extended his compliments and would like to invite Dr. Shaklee to golf and lunch, at his country club, that very morning. The invitation to meet the greatest inventor of them all topped any considerations. Still, in spite of his excitement at the thought of meeting the "Wizard of Menlo Park," Forrest wondered at this summons. Edison was known to place a very real value on his own time and it was recorded fact that he had kept visiting dignitaries waiting endlessly, rather than leave a project on which he was working. It was also known that he would spend whatever time was required on anyone, regardless of his station, if he believed that person could furnish him with a clue on a subject in which he was interested.

Forrest remembers his first meeting with Edison.[1] The inventor who was then 82 years of age, was something over 5' 9" in height, and had a bulky appearance. His face was benignly handsome. Forrest saw at once that Edison's touted indifference to clothes was not exaggerated. He was wearing a plain, dark suit with no particular styling. It was said that the inventor reordered his clothes by having a suit copied that he considered comfortable. On the rare occasions that he had allowed himself to be measured personally, the suits simply did not fit to his liking. Edison's blue-gray eyes were bright and curious, and in spite of his extreme deafness, he seemed to have no difficulty in conversing.

Forrest soon discovered that Edison was a poor golfer. Forrest's game at the time was in the upper 80's. "It seemed to me that he was shooting in the 190's poor fellow," says Dr. Shaklee.

After a while, Edison said, "Doc, are you enjoying this as much as I am?"

"Just about," Forrest replied anxious to stop since he had been hitting into the rough purposely to keep his score high.

"Then let's go have lunch," Edison said, leading the way into the club house. At the table they were joined once more

157

by Edison's secretary. Soft drinks were served, followed by a simple lunch. Although Edison claimed to be nutrition conscious, and indeed, ate rather sparingly, Forrest noted that the inventor topped off his lunch with pie and coffee with sugar. This was followed by a cigar. Edison who was seated between Forrest and his secretary, kept up a lively conversation. It amazed Forrest that the deaf man never hesitated in his responses. At first, Forrest assumed that Edison was an extraordinary lip reader, but he soon noticed that the inventor didn't seem to be looking at him at all. Finally, Forrest was alerted by a slight rustling of the tablecloth by their knees. Ostensibly to make himself more comfortable, Forrest slid back in his chair and gave a side-long glance at the edge of the table. Edison's secretary had his hand laid across one knee of his employer. That scene is described by Forrest, "any time I said a word I could see that hand going just like lightning—oh, he was fast—telegraph, Morse code—and Edison would answer right back almost as though he'd heard it, although I knew he couldn't hear thunder. And yet he wasn't looking at my lips because we were sitting side-by-side, but I can still look straight ahead and almost read a newspaper out of the side of my eyes. I could see that hand jiggle, jiggle, jiggle as fast as I was speaking."

Forrest remembers as well, at that first meeting, that Edison engaged in a wide variety of topics. Like Darrow, he had a rather low opinion of education. When he had first introduced the motion picture, he had looked upon it as a vehicle of education. He had not envisioned filmmaking as a source of entertainment, and when that was what it became, he lost interest in it, claiming that he was after all, a scientist not a theatrical producer. But, visual training via the medium of films was the future world of education, he believed.

He spoke openly of his attempts at reproducing rubber in the United States, and told Forrest that the Edison Botanic Research Corporation established two years earlier, had listed literally thousands of plants and had managed, by crossbreeding goldenrod weed, to produce a strain with high rubber content. But, h₁ ¹mitted that it was costly and the rubber was of inferior quality. He spoke of the close cooperation that he had received from his partners in the venture, Henry Ford and Harvey Firestone. Forrest must meet them, he suggested. Forrest nodded politely thinking that this was really just idle chatter and that nothing would come of it. Edison showed great interest in Forrest, his work and his ventures.

"He was a fascinating man to listen to," Forrest says, "but I tried not to divulge any more information than I had to because it's wise to keep an important man anxious."

Forrest honestly did not expect to see Edison again after that luncheon, and he was both delighted and surprised when the inventor invited him to visit his lab on the following day.

Chapter XVII

EDISON WELCOMED Forrest the next morning at his home on the bamboo-lined banks of the Caloosahatchee River. The plantation-style main building with colonnaded breezeways had been built in sections, transported to Fort Myers by ship, and assembled in 1886. Edison called his winter home, Seminole Lodge. The estate, some 13 or 14 acres which is now called Edison Park, was a maze of exotic horticulture developed more with an eye to experiment than aesthetics. Friends had sent him seedlings and croppings of unusual plants from their travels all over the world. In addition to the main house and guest accomodations, was a swimming pool, with a surprisingly modern lack of ornamentation, considering it was built in 1900. Edison had reinforced the pool with native bamboo rather than steel, and was proud of the fact that it had no cracks in it. The laboratory, roughly a hundred yards from the house was separated by a path, which later became McGregor Boulevard.

In his comfortable but unpretentious living room, the inventor shared coffee with his guest. The furnishings, if not spartan, were simple with obvious touches by Mina Edison reflected in chintz drapes and wicker armchairs. Edison pointed out his original carbon filament light bulbs, which were still being used, and the handmade brass chandelier designed in his own workshops.

On their way to the laboratory, Edison pointed out the adjoining estate which belonged to his friend Henry Ford. The gate which separated the two estates was never closed, he said. Outside the lab, a Banyan tree, which Harvey Firestone had brought to Edison from India, was flourishing. The Banyan, with its roots like sprawling arteries, is now, supposedly, the largest in Florida. In the laboratory itself,

160

Forrest noted machinery for the extraction of latex from Goldenrod weed. Edison conducted Forrest on a tour of the premises, patiently showing him each step of the process and explaining in detail what each of his technicians was working on.

At a point where Edison was looking through a microscope, Forrest noticed that two men had entered the lab. One of the men was alert, wiry, and in his middle sixties. Forrest recognized him at once as Henry Ford. The other was slight, with dark hair that had become grey and had a sandy-grey mustache. This man approached Edison stealthily, with mischief in his eyes. As Forrest looked up, he put a finger to his lips, cautioning him to silence. The man, who was Harvey Firestone, tiptoed up to Edison and tickled his ear with a timothy straw. Edison swiped at his ear impatiently, as if brushing away a fly. Firestone tickled again. And again, Edison swiped. Forrest noticed that Ford was having difficulty restraining his laughter.

Firestone continued tickling Edison's ear until finally the inventor swung around in annoyance, determined to catch the persistent fly. Upon seeing who his tormentor was, Edison gave a roar of laughter and pounced on Firestone. Whereupon, the octagenarian and Firestone, who was sixty-one, grappled each other and tussled on the floor. Forrest was fascinated. Rolling around on the lab floor like two street urchins were the greatest inventor of all times and one of the United States' most successful industrialists, while Ford, who was certainly the nation's most famous manufacturer, watched the proceedings with detached amusement. When the sporting was done, Edison introduced Forrest.

Recalling that meeting and his impressions of the automobile tycoon and the tire magnate, Forrest notes that Ford was aloof, almost austere and that Firestone seemed quite friendly. The veneration that Ford felt for Edison is well documented and indeed, when the group sat down to lunch that day, Ford recounted the episode which had

161

marked the turning point in his life. It was in 1895 when he was chief engineer at the Edison Illuminating Company in Detroit. At a company banquet, Ford was able to talk to Edison privately. He discussed his dream of a self-contained lightweight engine that could develop a high horsepower.

Edison encouraged him, telling Ford that he foresaw a great future for such an invention. Within a year, Ford had the beginnings of a workable vehicle. But, from the moment of Edison's prediction, Ford became his devoted admirer. It was a worship that did not end even with Edison's death in 1931. At the time that Forrest met him in 1929, Ford was Edison's neighbor in Fort Myers and Firestone lived in Miami. The three men were mutual partners in the Edison Botanical enterprises; naturally the subject of domestically-produced rubber came up. Now, Forrest found himself the center of interest, not only because of his synthetic rubber development, but for his touring home, which Ford considered ingenious. Forrest visited Edison on several occasions after that day, and, because he planned to spend the better part of that year in Florida, rented a cottage not far from the Edison estate.

On subsequent meetings, Forrest was strongly impressed by the sheer mental capacity of the inventor's mind. Edison was an inveterate reader. Forrest knew, of course, the story of how at the age of 21, Edison had studied the journals of the self-taught English scientist, Michael Faraday, and quickly learned to perform all of the electrical experiments described. Seated in the inventor's library, Forrest saw that Edison's reading tastes were eclectic, encompassing everything from the classics to popular magazines. And, Edison reconfirmed Forrest's attitude in several things—his need to keep abreast with the times and impatience with the past, which is expressed in the book, EDISON: HIS LIFE AND INVENTIONS, and which was written when Edison was 63 years old.

"I don't live with the past; I am living for today and

162

tomorrow. I am interested in every department of science, arts, and manufacture. I read all the time on astronomy, chemistry, biology, and physics, music, metaphysics, mechanics, and other branches—political economy, electricity, and, in fact, all things that are making for progress in the world. I get all the proceedings of the scientific societies, the principal scientific and trade journals, and read them. I also read "The Clipper," "The Police Gazette," "The Billboard," "The Dramatic Mirror," and a lot of similar publications, for I like to know what is going on. In this way I keep up to date, and live in a great moving world of my own, and, what's more, I enjoy every minute of it."[1]

Referring to some event of the past, he said: "Spilt milk doesn't interest me. I have spilt lots of it, and while I have always felt it for a few days, it is quickly forgotten, and I turn again to the future."

During another talk on kindred affairs, it was suggested to Edison that, as he had worked so hard all his life, it was about time for him to think somewhat of the pleasures of travel and the social side of life. He replied laughingly: "I already have a schedule worked out. From now until I am seventy-five years of age, I expect to keep more or less busy with my regular work, not, however, working as many hours or as hard as I have in the past. At seventy-five I expect to wear loud waistcoats with fancy buttons; also gaiter tops; at eighty I expect to learn how to play bridge, whist and talk foolishly to the ladies. At eighty-five I expect to wear a full-dress suit every evening at dinner, and at ninety—well, I never plan more than thirty years ahead."[2]

Those who have attended Forrest's lectures know that similar sentiments are expressed by him.

"To heck with yesterday, what's doing today?" says Forrest.

And, "Keep on keeping on." Their attitudes towards fail-

163

ure, as well, Forrest noted, were identical. Like Edison, Forrest never considered the impossible—so many wrong attempts merely drew him closer to the right approach. "I always want to know all the ways a project *can't* be done," Forrest maintains. "Each failure brings success all the nearer."

Thinker, reader, doodler and writer even in his last years, Edison contrasted sharply with his friend Ford. Ford, who in early life prided himself on his folksy image, was not a reader, loathed "big" words, and never kept notes. Besides his enormous legacy of 1,093 patents, Edison left diaries and virtually hundreds of notebooks covering a multitude of subjects. Although Ford was present at some of these encounters with Edison, Forrest found him a difficult man to warm to. Nevertheless, he concedes admiration for the manner in which Ford handled his detractors when he was ridiculed by the press. During the first World War, Ford had been persuaded to spearhead a Peace Ship venture, which was to end the war by Christmas, 1915. It was a time when pacifists were looked upon at best as crackpots and at worst as traitors. In an editorial, the *Chicago Tribune* excoriated Ford for his policies.

Ford sued the *Tribune* and during the trial, uttered his famous, "History is bunk. . ." comment. Although he won his case, Ford was awarded only six cents damages. The *Tribune's* high-powered attorneys managed to make Ford reveal his general ignorance. Forrest recalls that at one point Ford was asked what it was that made him think he was in a position to address himself to matters which were beyond the scope of his experience. Ford retorted with words to the effect that he might not have the brains to know all the answers, but that he had enough brains to hire people best capable of doing so.[3]

Ford believed that making money was synonymous with doing good. If you employed many people, paid them well and sold your product cheap enough for everyone to buy—then by doing that much good, you would attract all the money that you could ever use.[4]

But, Forrest points out that both Ford and Firestone were the first to raise pay standards and provide working benefits for their employees. The vast wealth that he accumulated inspired Ford to make his voice heard, with the result that he financed his own newspaper, the Dearborn Independent. Several blatantly anti-semitic articles brought additional criticism upon Ford, and he eventually abandoned the project.[5]

About nature, Ford once said, "We shall learn to be the masters rather than the servants of nature." As for Firestone, beyond their first meeting, Forrest never saw him again.

In the early autumn of 1929, Forrest heard from his patent attorney in Chicago. His request for his synthetic rubber patents was denied, because a patent for a similar product had been filed by Harvey Firestone.

Forrest makes no connection between his meetings with these men and the rejection of his patent application. Just as a group of scientists had worked simultaneously on the development of vitamins; just as Daimler and Benz in Germany, Panhard and De Dion in France, Napier in England and the Dureyea Brothers, Ford and others were working unknown to each other in the development of gasoline-propelled vehicles in the States.[6] So it was, he concludes, quite natural that the idea he assumed to be his alone, was being developed and perfected on many levels and by numerous people. Forrest has always maintained that "Thoughts are things. They circulate in the universe and they take possession of you, it's what you do with them that counts." This philosophy may have helped to ease his disappointment.

Since he had come to Florida for a vacation, Forrest decided it was time to enjoy it. He packed the family into the touring home and headed for the Everglades. They were gone for about three weeks. When he returned, Forrest learned for the first time of the stock market crash.

At first, Forrest was not too concerned since most of his

165

money was in bonds rather than stocks. It would be some time before the fate of his finances was established. Dreams of the ultra-modern scientific nutrition laboratory would once again have to be shelved. And, he would have to forget about continuing his research. Or would he? In essence, could he not start out again on a small scale and devote himself strictly to the study of nutrition? Wasn't it possible to develop nutritionally sound products and build from that? Forrest told himself that the only way he would ever know for sure was to give it his best try. So, while the bond companies were assessing what they could pay to their holders, Forrest mapped out his plans for the future.

From the time that he had been burned out of his clinic in the Cerro Gordo Hotel, Forrest's objective had been to scout the appropriate location for his laboratory. Their journey from Iowa had progressed into Texas, then across Louisiana and finally Florida. Now it seemed logical to encompass the rest of Florida, and up the eastern coast to see if there were a suitable place for establishing a research laboratory. But, Forrest admits, that even while doing so, there was an urge to go west. He discussed the decision with his wife and sons, and because the Northwest was still unspoiled and natural, the plan was for Forrest to establish his lab there.

They had made this decision in Miami and were heading back through Fort Myers. It was a winter evening, and as they drove along the Tamiami Trail past Edison's estate, a familiar figure stepped off the curb. In the waning light, Forrest tooted and waved. Edison, recognizing the vehicle, stepped back on the curb and gave the Shaklees a brisk military salute. The touring home trundled past the great inventor on its adventure into the future.

Chapter XVIII

IN THE SUMMER of 1930, the gallant Shaklee touring home entered Bellingham in Washington State. To the mid-western Shaklees, it seemed that the west must signify sunshine and balmy weather which they had experienced enroute, in both Southern and Northern California. They were not prepared for the mist and rain in Bellingham. For two weeks it rained incessantly, which was enough to make Forrest decide that he did not want to live there. The wheels rolled again, this time through Portland and Eugene to Medford, Oregon, where it was oppressively hot. Forrest gave it three days, before deciding to return to Eugene.

By now, the family was exhausted from travelling, and Forrest assessed that Eugene embodied many of the things that he was seeking. Primarily, there was a good university, and with his two sons to educate, this was an important feature. The land was rich with vegetation, which meant that he could experiment with a wide variety of shrubs and herbs. Land was reasonable and the mountains and streams provided recreation and fishing. Despite the rain, Forrest decided to settle there with his family. The bond companies had paid off on his assets. He had received ten cents on the dollar. From being, if not rich, at least comfortably well off, Forrest now had a very reduced nest egg. He built a modest laboratory with minimal equipment, rented a cottage for his family, and began work. That winter it rained almost daily. Water pattered on the roof of his lab, dripped from the boughs of the trees and sloshed as he drove to and from work. The mist, the rain, seemed part of everything. The constant sound of drizzling pursued Forrest, to the point where he became depressed.

At the end of the year, he admitted to his family that

despite some of its advantages, he did not want to remain in Eugene. He remembered while travelling in Northern California, they had gone through a city with a charming lake in the middle of it. The memory of the place had stayed with him. Consulting his travel notes, he found that the city was called Oakland.

On July 4, 1931, the Shaklee Family arrived in Northern California. Homes to rent were plentiful after the crash, and Forrest found one on seventeen acres in Walnut Creek. The owner of the house, a former president of a building loan organization which had gone under, had been obliged to give it up. The acreage was given over mostly to prune orchards. It was an attractive setting, but Forrest knew that he had to face the inescapable truth. He would have to go back into practice. The settlement from his bonds was dwindling fast and there was no other alternative. Now, he had to pool all of his resources, financial as well as material, to begin again from the ground up.

It made sense to him, to reestablish the formula that had proven successful in the past. So, the Shaklee Clinic opened in the Ray Building on Broadway in Oakland. The operation consisted of multi-service medical care, with a staff of medical specialists and chiropractors. Gradually, the clinic grew and Forrest developed another lucrative practice.

To anyone, without the stubborn drive of Forrest Shaklee, it would have seemed patently clear, that his destiny lay in his chiropractic and administrative skills. But, Forrest was consumed by a nagging inner dictum. In a world that was hurtling towards technological progress; where everything edible seemed to be sprayed, processed, preserved or packaged, in one form or another, he longed for the purity of natural food. What he saw in Oakland markets were oversized handsome vegetables, harvested while they were green; cucumbers and apples sleek in their wax coatings; and pallid hot-house tomatoes. He wondered about the nutrient values of such foods. How much was retained? What were the time factors between harvesting, shipment to the grocer and purchase by the consumer? Even in taste, they were a far cry from the freshly spaded vegetables and freshly laid eggs of the farms in Iowa. Of course, he realized that there were farms in California and that fresh produce was available to them, but when did that produce get to the consumer? And, he was bothered by the wide range of insecticides that were being used. Certain poultry, such as capons, were being injected with hormones to create plump breasts. What was happening to the natural content of vitamins and minerals? What was happening to Nature?

Urged by these thoughts, Forrest began regimens of food supplementation with his patients. Once again, the proven Shaklee formulas were compounded and supplied to the patients. And, again, Forrest, Jr., now a high school student, along with Raleigh who was ten, assisted by filling capsules at night after they had completed their homework.

Forrest began to find that people were interested in his theories on nutrition. He was invited to lecture on the subject. Using the oratory skills he had inherited from his grandfather, David, and those that he had acquired by watching Bryan, Forrest drew capacity houses at his lectures.

It was also a time of study for Forrest. In 1930, he attained his degree of Philosopher of Chiropractic from the West Coast Chiropractic College. The following year he received his diploma as Doctor of Naturopath from the California Chiropractic College. In 1935, he instructed biochemistry at the same college.

To mitigate the routines of his practice, Forrest actualized his long-standing interest in Masonic rites, and joined the Oakland Scottish Rite Bodies, Aahmes Shrine of Oakland and the So-Al-Co Shrine Club.

The interest in art and history imbued in Forrest by Dr. Lindley so many years earlier in Davenport, was re-awakened when he became a member of both the Oakland museum and the California Historical Society. It was a full life and, in the material sense, a successful one. But, in the recesses of his mind there was the conviction that this was not entirely what he wanted to do with his life.

In many ways a conventional man, Forrest could not simply unshackle himself of his responsibilities, say, in the manner of Gauguin, who abandoned his professional career, wife and family to go to Tahiti and paint. Admittedly, Gauguin knew he could paint—and he knew that Tahiti was where he wanted to work. Even had Forrest been morally capable of denying his commitments, he had, as yet, no clear picture of *how* he could bring the products he was continually developing, to the general public. He has never—and does not to this day—consider himself a businessman. Being unencumbered by this stereotype, has allowed him latitude which characterizes his genius in business. For example: In the annual volume of business at the clinic, there were the usual number of patients who defaulted on their bills. Rather than follow the standard procedure of reminder statements and, finally, dunning letters, Forrest made the unpaid bills a Christmas gift. By the middle of December, all delinquent accounts were stacked on Forrest's desk. On each, Forrest wrote a personal note in which he said words to the effect that he hoped he had rendered satisfactory services, and that since it was a time of goodwill towards men, he was enclosing a receipt of the unpaid balance marked paid in full. More than fifty percent of these delinquent bills were subsequently paid outright, and a fair number of patients came into the office to make arrangements for time payments.

When one of these patients was questioned by Forrest as to why he was paying his bill, after Forrest had cancelled it, the patient responded, "because your way of doing business made me want to feel like an honest man."

Forrest admits that he had no idea of what prompted his action. "I just felt that if they couldn't pay, I didn't want them to suffer over it—the only decent attitude, it seemed to me. So, while I don't think of myself as a smart business man, this one particular way of handling it was the smart way to do it," then, with a characteristic chuckle, "Got a

170

darned sight more out of 'em, then any dunning credit agency could."

Should anyone think, despite his claims to non-business, that Forrest can be easily deceived, an earlier episode proves the opposite.

While Forrest was practicing in Mason City, many of his patients were farmer families. Those were the days of house calls and, since these people lived in rural areas, the distance was often over fifty miles. Numerous calls came at night and in freezing weather. On one such night, Forrest received a call from a very successful hog farmer. His daughter was having severe pains in her back. Other doctors had tried to alleviate the pain, but to no avail. Forrest made the trip and adjusted the young woman's spine. She felt immediate relief. He made several follow-up calls, until he was satisfied that his patient was fully recovered. The farmer expressed his gratitude, but when the statements were mailed, he simply ignored them. When Forrest's secretary called the farmer's home, he became abusive. This perplexed Forrest. It was not a case of hardship; the farmer had excellent standing in his community. Forrest then mailed him a final notice saying that the bill would be put into the hands of a collection agency.

This brought an irate call from the farmer, who said that he didn't like that kind of notice and ended his conversation with, "I'll tell you this, Dr. Shaklee, if you get that money before I do, you let me know!"

"All right," Forrest replied, "I'll do that."

As it happened, the sheriff in whose county the farm was located, was also Forrest's patient. The farmer whose first name was Jim, was well known to the sheriff. "Doc," said the sheriff, "Jim's as good as gold and you'll never lose a dollar on him. But he doesn't pay for services sometimes for three or four years. Does business on the other guy's money. Smart," the sheriff tapped his head knowingly.

"The answer to that kind of smart, is to outsmart!" replied Forrest.

In the course of their talk, Forrest learned that Farmer Jim was getting ready to ship several hundred head of hogs. Forrest asked the sheriff to call him at the time when the hogs were to be delivered to the buyer. Shortly after, the sheriff phoned and said, "Jim is hauling in a whole trainload of hogs and the buyer is here to take delivery."

Forrest had, in the meantime, secured a lien against the payment for the hogs which he had placed in the hands of the sheriff.

When Farmer Jim had delivered his hogs and went to pick up his draft from the buyer, the sheriff presented the court order confiscating payment. Enraged, the farmer phoned Forrest.

"Damn it Doc you know you're holding up thousands of dollars for a measly medical bill."

"Yes," Forrest replied calmly. "I've thought of that, but it's been kind of hard to get my message across. Thought you might need a jolt. Besides, you told me to let you know if I got that money before you did. Well, I have. Your draft will be in escrow until I get paid."

Farmer Jim paid up promptly, what's more, he eventually saw the humor of the situation and continued as a patient. Only, each time he or a member of his family was treated, he'd pay at once.

"I got a great deal of satisfaction in carrying out his instructions," Forrest recalls.

Between his practice, teaching assignments and lectures, Forrest was kept busy and time passed. A decade had gone by since he had first hung his shingle in the Oakland office. He was repairing the losses that he had experienced in the crash.

Life for the Shaklees in 1941 was serene. Forrest, Jr., who had taken bio-chemistry and accounting at the University of California, Berkeley, was working towards his own accounting business. Raleigh, who by now was called Lee, was in his junior year at U.C. Berkeley. He had for several years been interested in radio technology and was a ham radio enthusiast. Ruth had made a fine adjustment to her life in California, and was an excellent homemaker for her husband and sons. Then, in an instant, the serenity was shattered.

It was a summer day and Ruth was shopping on 11th Street in downtown Oakland. As she was crossing the street with the light, a driver raced through the crosswalk. Several pedestrians were hit. Ruth was critically injured. She lingered for several months, while a battery of doctors fought to save her. The internal damage was beyond repair and she passed away. The driver was young, drunk and uninsured. In the midst of the desolate prospect of Christmas without wife and mother, the three Shaklee men heard the news of the bombing of Pearl Harbor.

Chapter XIX

ALWAYS CLOSE, the father and sons were drawn into an even tighter bond after Ruth's passing. But, with the war, the sons felt impelled to serve their country. In January of 1942, Lee enlisted in the Navy. At twenty-one, lithe and boyishly handsome, Lee looked every bit like the idealized sailors portrayed by Sinatra and Kelly in an MGM musical. His radio buff experience came in handy, and he was signed on as a radioman and shipped to the Northwest coast of New Guinea. At the time, the only area that the United States held in New Guinea was Milne Bay, at the extreme eastern tip. Lee recalls those times with a wry smile. "It was a very gung-ho war—and, of course, I was going to save the world. I mean, if the Navy needed radio technicians—well, then, they *had* to have me!"

In New Guinea, Lee was assigned to a patrol torpedo boat detail, operating out of the Morobe river, one of the advance bases at that time. The PT boats functioned at night and, when not in action, they were deployed to various hiding places along the river banks and camouflaged with netting. This was, of course, to avoid detection by Japanese bombers who made periodic raids.

PT boats were extremely vulnerable, since they were basically speedboats with plywood hulls and two torpedoes on each side. They relied for their function, on speed and selected armaments. The power, provided by three 750 HP Packard marine engines, allowed the boat to build up speed, then lift up on a plane and skim across the surface of the water, reaching up to 45 knots. This, Lee says, "is pretty close to fifty miles an hour and fast enough to run away from anything at sea."

The PT boat to which Lee was originally assigned was used to scout barges, which the Japanese used to bring in additional troops. The barges, which moved slowly by comparison, would use machine-gun fire on the fast moving PT boats.

It was in this type of skirmish that Lee saw a great deal of action. The PT boats were armed with twin turrets, each mounted with a pair of 50-caliber machine guns. In addition, Lee was assigned to a 33mm machine gun on the right hand side of the cockpit. Generally, Lee felt that this extra armament was incidental.

"If you've got four of the 50 caliber machine guns blasting a stream of bullets, some armour piercing, some tracers, others of the shrapnel explosive type, they can just disintegrate the side of the barge. And, disintegrate some of the crew, too, I must admit."

In the war, there is a fine line between valor and extreme risk, and around 1943, Lee was assigned to a skipper who was famed for his daredevil exploits. This was Lieutenant John D. Bulkeley, who had achieved reknown early in the war as the skipper of the motor torpedo that had evacuated General MacArthur from Corregidor and had run him clear down through the Phillippines to Australia. Bulkeley became the Commander in Chief of the squadron of PT boats operating in New Guinea. While Bulkeley might have been overly zealous in combat, his administrative planning skills can be attested to by the fact that he chose his crew with great deliberation. In reviewing files on radiomen, he learned that because of Lee's ham radio training, Lee could most efficiently set up and work the radio communications equipment, and so he had him transferred to his own boat.

In order to do battle against heavily-armed shore installations, the PT boat was fitted with a 20mm cannon on the fantail. To accommodate the extra weight, decks had to be reinforced, and struts and beams were added in the engine room as support. Another reason for the cannon was to provide added fire power against pursuing destroyers and cruisers. But, the weight of the cannon created a serious problem. No longer could the boat rise and plane the surface of the water, and the speed was cut drastically. Now, if pursued by destroyers, the PT boat could no longer fire its torpedoes and race from the scene. Instead it would be obliged to fight back against the heavily armed ships. "Not a very equitable situation," Lee recalls.

It was a similar circumstance in which a young skipper from the same PT boat squadron found himself. Although Lee never met him, John F. Kennedy's PT boat was also under Lt. Bulkeley's command. The Kennedy PT 109 incident occurred when the Japanese destroyer, Amagiri ran it down. The vessel on which Lee was Chief Radioman fared better, although it went through its share of risks and perils. Bulkeley was fearless and, according to Lee, would fight when others would run. When firing on shore installations, Bulkeley would bring the boat perilously close to the point where the crew feared as much from the dangers of the hull of their boat being ripped by coral reefs, as they did the firing.

Lee points out a phenomenon of those battles. "A peculiarity of war, which Americans basically understood and which baffled the Japanese, was the principle of the moving target. The Japanese simply couldn't understand that they were supposed to shoot ahead and let the boat catch up with the bullets."

In the night, the crew could see the Japanese tracers falling behind the PT boat as they made their escape.

"Fortunately for us with our dead-weight cannon and lessened speed, we never got into a race against the Japanese destroyers." But, he recalls those times, fraught as they were with the danger of imminent death, as most intensely exciting. "I was at that age when you can't conceive of your mortality. The next guy maybe—but not you." Smilingly, Lee admits, "I still feel that way."

With Lee in the service and his older son anxious to join, Forrest began to speculate how he could contribute to the war effort and still keep his options open. So, while continuing to work at the clinic, he began an intensive course in radio theory and code practice for submarines. Upon becoming a licensed shortwave radio operator, Forrest was assigned to submarine duty as a civilian scientific researcher.

Forrest and the other civilian radio technicians assisted in the training of radio operators for submarines. This time, there was talk of a commission, but Forrest declined it preferring his civilian status.

With his father busily engaged in his submarine radio work and his full-time practice, Forrest, Jr. now felt he was able to join the war effort. At twenty-four, Forrest, Jr. was a clear-eyed, brisk young man, with a warm easy-going manner. He bore a remarkable resemblance to his father. Versatile, Forrest, Jr. liked nothing better than relaxing after auditing chores by singing in barbershop quartets. He had a fine bass voice and was much in demand. From his great-grandfather, David Overton, he had inherited a talent for guns, particularly small arms. Based on Forrest, Jr.'s university studies in bio-chemistry, the Army, with uncharacteristic perceptiveness, assigned him to the medical corps. This was soon rectified when Forrest, Jr. received orders to report to Fort Sill, Oklahoma where he was given basic training in gun mechanics, for 105mm and 155mm cannons.

Next, he was assigned to a military cadre to teach small arms. In this capacity, Forrest, Jr. had a chance to excel and was a very capable instructor.

One day during the latter part of the war, Forrest, Jr. was dispatched to the personnel building where he found himself in the company of over fifty men. The Major in charge eventually called Forrest, Jr.'s name and handed him his orders. He was to be technical administrator to the recruiting officer, and as such, was the only assigned man on the post, unattached to any particular battalion.

Forrest, Jr. soon found that the Recruiting Section, while not given the exalted treatment of top military brass, enjoyed a privileged status. So as not to interfere with the

177

momentum of recruiting, the word came down that the recruiting staff were to be excused from such banes of Army life as KP, guard duty and overseas shipment lists. Because of his previous work experience as a disc jockey, radio announcer and scriptwriter, Forrest, Jr.'s work was mainly recruiting public relations. In this capacity, he was responsible for writing all public address announcements, press releases and radio spots promoting recruiting.

One of Forrest, Jr.'s regular assignments was to pick up the form 20 folders of the men awaiting reassignment. These folders were located near the Old Fort Sill, and was four Army blocks away from the recruiting office. "This," in Forrest, Jr.'s words, "translates to a long walk." Next to the Old Fort Sill, were the casual barracks. Here, officers who were awaiting reassignment were billeted. To while away the time, walking back to the recruiting office, Forrest, Jr. would read the form 20 folders. One evening while engrossed in one of these files, Forrest heard an abrupt shout, "Corporal!"

It was a Second Lieutenant, whom Forrest had not noticed. After upbraiding Forrest for neglecting to salute an officer, the Lieutenant said that he was citing him for insubordination.

Some time later, a jeep arrived at the Recruiting Office and Forrest, Jr. was whisked away to the Judge Advocate's Office. The Staff Judge Advocate, a full Colonel, and a man of obvious understanding, put Forrest, Jr. at ease immediately. A call was sent out over the PA system for the officer who had made the charge. While they waited for the Lieutenant, the colonel offered Forrest, Jr. a drink (which he declined), told him to loosen his tie, and suggested a game of cribbage. In the middle of the game, the door opened and the young Lieutenant, who had clearly forgotten his charge against Forrest, Jr. came in looking distraught.

Without glancing up from the game, the Colonel asked the Lieutenant, if Forrest, Jr. was the Corporal he had cited for insubordination. The Lieutenant, relaxing somewhat, said "yes," neglecting to add "Sir."

"Lieutenant, what is this insignia on my sleeve?"

"An eagle," replied the now completely flustered officer.

"And what does that make me?"

"A full Colonel—*sir!*"

"Correct. And until this minute you did not address me as sir—nor did you salute when you came into this room. Would you like me to prefer charges against you?"

"No *Sir!*" replied the officer.

"And would you like to drop your charges against this man?"

"Yes, *Sir!*"

"Thank you Lieutenant."

In 1943, Dr. Shaklee decided that he was going to retire and he began to wind down his practice. He had decided not to sell the clinic because he wanted to be sure that his patients would not fall into some regimen beyond his control. The Shaklee name would not serve as an umbrella for someone else's techniques. So, he paid five month's advance rent on his offices and replaced his shingle with a sign that said simply, "Retired."

Once again, Forrest found himself financially able to do as he pleased. And, it pleased him to retire from the rigors of dealing with patients in pain. But, as usual, retirement to Forrest was not synonymous with inactivity, and he began to scout around for a new avocation. This he found on a ranch of 420 acres, situated thirteen miles from Willets, California, just east of the game refuge. The asking price per acre was $114.00. The property was far enough from the city of Oakland, that Forrest felt he could be isolated from his former patients, who were unwilling to accept the fact of his retirement.

Before closing the deal, Forrest carefully surveyed the land which was represented as having no water supply. But, certain moist areas which he discovered when wading through brush and weeds as high as his head, convinced him

179

that there was water on the site.

A further search uncovered the presence of an 18-inch curbed well, which tapped an underground river. This well had been used some fifteen or twenty years earlier for irrigation purposes. This was all Forrest needed to know to make him buy the property.

At once he installed a 12-inch pump for flooding and created ponds for ducks and geese. Next, he erected a wooden lodge with a tarred roof, nothing pretentious, simply a place where hunters could gather in reasonable comfort. The clubroom's dimensions were ample, thirty by thirty-six feet. A hand pump provided drinking water, but there was no such nicety as running water. There was, in addition, a cabin that could sleep thirty-two men in bunks. A smaller cabin provided accommodations for four; this was usually reserved for married couples. While there were adequate toilet facilities in the clubhouse, the cabins had to rely on an outhouse. With typical Shaklee whimsy, the sign on the outhouse read, "First Natural Bank—Time depositors only."

The Hunting Lodge, generously supplied with fowl that flew over the game refuge or swam in the ponds, was an immediate success. Frequent visitors were comedians Bob Hope and Andy Devine. It was for a time, the ideal respite for Forrest, a return to nature and a regrouping of his resources. Within three years, the property had so greatly increased in value, that in 1945, he sold it for $500 an acre to a cattle rancher.

On the surface, it would seem that Forrest had simply capitalized on a good investment and taken his profit. But, what caused him to sell his ranch was something more deep seated. For all his protestations of being tired of patients and exhausted from his practice, Forrest had never really abandoned either. To those who diligently tracked him down, Forrest made his services available. And, for those who clamored for their vitalized minerals, and the other products that had been part of their nutritional program, Forrest began compounding again.

And again, he was seized by the same dictate that told him of the growing need for nutritional supplements—a need that was very close to becoming, if not heralded, at least recognized. For it was during the war that the government established the first required daily allowances of vitamins and minerals, as a means of making certain that both the armed forces and the citizenry would be getting a certain measurable standard of nutrition. It was a thin crack of light, but it was all the illumination that Forrest required to kindle his deepest convictions. It would take him over ten years to put his dream into action.

Chapter XX

IN 1919 while Forrest was creating headlines as the first doctor in Iowa to fly to his patients' relief, a Canadian family visited the United States. Retired cattleman, William Potter, his British-born wife, Meithell Amanda, affectionately called Minty, and their pretty teenaged daughter, Dorothy, had arrived in San Francisco. Potter was planning a tour of California and Mexico to determine where he wanted to settle with his family. For this purpose, a car was being delivered in San Francisco.

Potter started as a young telegrapher and station master with the Canadian Pacific Railroad. Being an aggressive young man, Potter was soon promoted to the position of developer of a new townsight in the upper country. The new town was to be named Nicola. The Canadian Pacific Railroad was extending its tracks from Vancouver up the Frazer Canyon, to Spencer's Bridge, across the river and up to the little city of Merritt, then on to the new proposed town of Nicola.

The station was built, the railroad completed; the occasion called for a jubilant celebration, attended by officials and dignitaries.

Potter's duties were not confined to that of stationmaster alone. He soon made investments in leases of large acreages—raising cattle and thoroughbred horses.

The town of Nicola boasted of two hotels, four churches, a post office, schoolhouse, a courthouse and many residences, among them, Potter's new home. Potter was part owner of the stage line, which also delivered mail to the rural areas. Shortly after their marriage, Minty announced that she was pregnant. As the day of delivery approached, William, alarmed that his gentle-born wife would not have the proper care in Nicola, sent her to Vancouver to await delivery.

But, Dorothy took her time in coming into this world, and was two weeks late. And, as Forrest jokingly says, "She's been late ever since."

Within a few years, Potter considered his financial position satisfactory and retired at the age of forty-three. He moved his family to the little city of Duncan, on Vancouver Island. There he purchased a farm, and became a Gentleman Farmer. Dorothy graduated from Duncan High School.

The Potters, when they arrived in San Francisco in early 1919, were amazed at the sight of the San Franciscans wearing hygiene masks. The flu epidemic that raged through Europe and America had not yet reached Canada.

The tour down the California coast got as far as Tijuana, Mexico, when Minty, taking one look at the bordertown squalor, put her very proper English foot down. "Mexico," she concluded, "was no place to bring up a young girl." It had seemed to her, that the Bay Area in Northern California had all the elements conducive to their plans for a suitable home. In particular she remembered, (as Forrest was later to do) an enchanting lake in the middle of the town. If Lake Merritt in Oakland had a familiar ring for the Potters, it was because the town in which Potter had become a successful cattle rancher, had been called Merritt, in the Nicola Valley.

Mrs. Potter, named after a certain Lady Meithell, had been born in Rugley, Staffordshire, England, and reared by her mother on an estate owned by the Marquis of Angelsey. Minty wanted to be sure that her only child would derive the full benefit of her heritage. These were the traditions of becoming an accomplished horsewoman, and, of course, the deportment befitting a young lady.

Oakland, just after World War I, and before the industry boom occasioned by World War II, was ideal in its gentle and still almost rural character. Learning from her mother, who rode sidesaddle, Dorothy became a skilled equestrienne, and rode regularly at Miss Graham's Riding Academy, in Oakland. And while, even today, Dorothy exudes the gregarious-

183

ness associated with Americans, the British filament of tradition and manners is evident.

Nor was her mother content to be the idle housewife of a retired man. From the time she had left England to visit her sister in Canada where she had met Potter, Minty had led a spirited life.

In California, while Dorothy was attending school, Minty turned her hand to business, was associated with the Allied Properties, and elected President of the Women's Chapter of the Hotel Greeters Association of California. She was known by, and in turn knew, every hotel owner in the State.

It seemed wise to the Potters to prepare their daughter for a career. So, upon graduating from high school, Dorothy attended the Polytechnical Business College in Oakland. At this time, the Potters received news of a devastating flood that had completely destroyed their home and practically all of the town of Nicola.

In the 1940's, Dorothy's training and skill had paid off and she was now office manager for a group of doctors. A member of the Eastern Star, and many young peoples' social clubs, her social life was full. To look at Dorothy, one can clearly appreciate that there must have been many suitors. Her warmth and gaiety, her genuine concern for everyone, to say nothing of a radiant complexion and bright-eyed prettiness, brought her considerable male attention. But, Dorothy knew that what she wanted was something very simple; very old fashioned. It had to do with a serious heart. And, she was content to wait rather than compromise.

Fate has more quirks than fiction will allow, and long before she ever met the man she would ultimately marry, Dorothy had occasion to get some inkling of what he was like. In late 1942, Dorothy was managing the office of a doctor located in the Ray Building.

The janitor of the building, whose name was Manuel, had been telling Dorothy about the terraced roof garden of a certain doctor, who grew all kinds of plants and herbs, it seemed, without soil. The plant garden, according to Manuel, was a sight truly worth seeing, and he suggested that someday he would show it to her. A month or so later, Dorothy met Manuel in the elevator. Manuel told her that since the doctor was closing his practice and probably wasn't in the office, they could go up and see his rooftop plant garden.

As Manuel had described it, the roof garden was tiered with boxes overflowing with greenery and vegetables. There were large trays of sprouts, some lacy with green tips, some clear with yellow beans, and they were growing in white ocean sand. These were alfalfa and mung bean sprouts. In other boxes there were clearly recognizable vegetables— carrots, onions, radishes and even lettuce. These, too, were growing without fertile soil, but in the sea sand. A sign said, "Dr. Shaklee's Experimental Garden."

Many years later, Dorothy learned that Forrest had grown his organic vegetable garden by using vitalized minerals to fertilize the sand.

With the war ended, Forrest resumed his programs of study. For many years the basic credo, What you think, you look; what you think, you do; what you think, you are—had engaged his imagination. He had kept copious notes on a variety of subjects to which this principle could be applied. Forrest developed the title, "Thoughtsmanship," which seemed to best embody the principle, and had begun a series of articles. These articles later became manuals which earned him a doctorate in philosophy. In 1947, he became the founder and President of the Shaklee Foundation, with the name "Thoughtsmanship" copyrighted.

Returning from service, both Forrest, Jr. and Lee were plunged into directing their energies towards business futures. Forrest, Jr., after a stint in sales, radio and public relations work, where he developed a natural proclivity for showmanship, settled into his own accounting firm.

Lee, foreseeing the possibilities of insurance sales, had established a foothold in that business, and by the late forties was a rising young executive.

Dr. Shaklee had been a lonely widower for seven years. Not that he had been without many opportunities to meet eligible women—on the contrary. His host of patients had no end of charming single sisters, mothers, and even daughters who would instantly bring joy and order into his presumably empty life. Forrest developed an instinct for these situations and became skilled at avoiding the planned introductions. He knew that, if and when the right woman came into his life, he would recognize her. And, with all the work that he had amassed for himself, he was busy enough and felt relatively happy.

But, matchmakers by necessity are an indomitable breed and come in all disguises. Little did Forrest suspect when he was having some clothes tailored, that the man responsible for his sartorial appearance would also be the only matchmaker to succeed. The tailor, Joe Smith, also produced suits for the doctors in the Latham Square Building where Dorothy now worked. In that capacity, Smith was a frequent visitor at the office, and while waiting to fit the doctors, he would pass the time with Dorothy. When he felt that he knew her sufficiently well, he asked the matchmaker's infallible question, "Well, Dorothy, what's a nice girl like you doing, not married?" Dorothy's response, "I'm perfectly happy the way I am," fell on deaf ears, and Joe was forever suggesting likely prospects. Of Forrest, he told Dorothy, "he'd be just the man for you." Finally, Dorothy was obliged to say, "Joe, please don't bother, I prefer to pick my own friends." Not to be outdone, Smith began badgering Forrest. But, Forrest came directly to the point with his tailor-cum-matchmaker. "I have had an objective for many years and until I achieve that, I don't want to tie myself down to home life again."

At that time, Forrest was living in what was once the Little Estate. He had an attractive suite with a front window facing Mosswood Park on the North. This was before the days that the trees and hedges were cleared off to make a picnic ground. It was a tranquil and ideal setting for the writing and planning which occupied his time. He had adjusted to life alone and was quite sure that that was what he wanted for the time being.

On a Wednesday afternoon, Forrest was walking along Telegraph Avenue, on his way to the bank, when he ran into Joe Smith. Seizing the opportunity and Forrest's arm, Joe said that since Wednesday was the doctor's day off in Dorothy's office, what better time to go up and meet the young lady?

Forrest protested that he had business at the bank.

"I'll go with you," Joe persisted.

Thinking that he would once and for all get rid of the man's pestering, Forrest agreed to go up and meet Dorothy. They found the offices closed and Dorothy, who was catching up on her work, was locked in her private office.

Although extremely busy, Dorothy ushered them in politely. Forrest noted the spontaneous friendliness, realizing that she thought he was a pharmaceutical salesman, some friend of Joe's who needed to list a call on his route sheet, and he was doubly impressed by her kindliness. Also, Dorothy was wearing a red dress that emphasized her vivid coloring. His mother, Martha, he remembered had always been partial to red dresses. No sooner were they seated, than Joe jumped to his feet, made some pretext about an appointment, and said that he would return shortly. Learning that Dorothy was originally from Canada, Forrest told her that he had just returned from a hunting trip there. In the midst of the conversation the phone rang. Dorothy answered and Joe's booming voice came over the receiver so loudly, that Forrest could hear every word.

"This is the doctor, I've been telling you about. Well, what do think of him?" Joe boomed.

Dorothy recalls that moment, "I felt myself getting as red as my dress. I wanted the floor to open up and swallow me." But, Forrest remembers that she handled the conversation adriotly, particularly since Joe said, "OK, well I won't be

187

coming back—tell Doc!"

"Oh, thank you," Dorothy replied, "I'll tell him." It was only then that Dorothy realized that Forrest was not a detail man. Partly because of her obvious embarrassment, but more due to the fact that he found Dorothy charming, Forrest suggested that he would like to repay her kindness for the visit, by inviting her to dinner sometime. Normally, Dorothy had a firm rule about giving out her home phone number, but to this day, Forrest teases her about the fact that she gave him both her office *and* her home phone number.

It was nearly a month before he used either. Immediately after that meeting, Forrest went on a three-week hunting trip. Upon his return there was a message from an old friend who lived in the East. Barry Hopkins (his radio name) was a radio personality for the National Broadcasting Company. Some years earlier, he had worked for Forrest as an office manager in one of his clinics. Hopkins and his wife were visiting California and wanted Forrest to dine with them—and naturally bring a date.

By the time Forrest called, Dorothy had just about forgotten the incident, although she confesses to being a little piqued at first, when she did not hear from him.

The evening spent together had all the components of right chemistry for both Forrest and Dorothy. Rather than a chance situation of being thrown together, Forrest realized that he wanted to see her often, and she reciprocated the feeling. But, Forrest's life objectives were for once becoming both clearer and closer and Dorothy, too, had her commitments. Her father had died and Minty had retired and was living with her. If this budding relationship could be nurtured with time, there was every indication that it would become permanent.

By then, Dorothy knew that Forrest wanted more than anything else, to apply the Shaklee name to a meaningful project. And, because quite simply he was the man she had been waiting for, she was content to try and help him achieve his aims without making any demands of him.

Part V

REALIZATION

Chapter XXI

WITH HIS retirement from practice, and after selling the ranch, the demands for Forrest as a lecturer grew. His appearances at Ebell Hall, the Women's City Club, and the auditorium of the Leamington Hotel, drew packed audiences. Even in the early fifties, the appeal to conformance with nature made sense to a growing number of people. Woven through the talks was the thread of Forrest's simple and workable "Thoughtsmanship" philosophy.

Dorothy proved an able and energetic assistant who spent evenings after work and on weekends, scouring the mailing lists that Forrest had developed in his practice, and sending out circulars and programs.

In 1951, Forrest had published four volumes on "Thoughtsmanship": These were; "Thoughtsmanship for Well Being," "Thoughtsmanship in Love and Marriage," "Thoughtsmanship for the Bride," and "Thoughtsmanship for the Salesman." The publication of this body of work earned for Forrest a doctorate in philosophy from the Commonwealth University in Los Angeles.

Throughout this book, we have discussed Dr. Shaklee's philosophy in regard to his life and his work. But, we have not identified the philosophy other than by terminology. We have spoken of The Golden Rule and Cooperation with Nature, under the aegis of "Thoughtsmanship." In one of those early works, "Thoughtsmanship in Love and Marriage," Forrest expresses some of the workings of "Thoughtsmanship" in relation to love.

"Love may be divided into three phases: spiritual, intellectual, and physical. Fortunate is the couple whose marriage is based upon all three phases. Theirs is a nearly perfect union. If your marriage is lacking one or more of these qualifications, don't give up and seek a divorce. It may not be too late to correct your weaknesses. Spiritual love can be awakened; soul love can be developed; and physical attraction can be restored. Through the production of creative thought, you can give intelligent direction to the expression of your love. I have seen thoughtsmanship miraculously change the lives of many discontented people and bring love and happiness into the home. It will do as much for you, if you will use your power of thought as outlined in these pages.

"Before we can determine the proper method of expressing our love, we must determine its origin. As we have outlined in previous messages, the Spark of Life, Spirit, or whatever name you wish to give it, is an endowment of the Creator. It expresses the life force within our body, controls the function of our organs, glands, etc. It supplies the motivating power that allows us to move about. Being a part of the Creative Intelligence, it possesses and expresses intelligence far beyond that of the soul-consciousness. The job of operating so intricate a machine as our body is too much for mere human intelligence, so we content ourselves with the knowledge that our physical functions are being directed by a force from within.

"We do not care to use any specific name in describing this endowment of the Creative Intelligence, so

190

we will simply call it the inner-consciousness. Our inner-consciousness is a pretty important factor in our life, for it is that which gives us life. It is the seat of our emotions and the custodian of our memory archives. It gives physical expression to the thoughts produced through the process of mind as directed by the soul, or it may act independently of the soul-intelligence, and often does in the case of an emergency.

"When we speak of soul-consciousness, we mean you. You do not possess a soul; you ARE a soul. You communicate with your inner-consciousness through the process of mind. The process of mind is produced by the brain; but the brain is only a physical organ and functions according to the directions given to it, just as does the heart, stomach, liver, and all other tissues of the body. The soul-consciousness records it in the storehouse of memory. That thought may be acted upon at once and given physical expression, or it may be stored in memory and be given expression at some later date. As, for instance, when we find ourselves doing a thing we haven't thought about for days, weeks, or even years. We call it habit, but habits are the effect of thoughts.

"Soul-consciousness having the power to produce thought can, therefore, produce thoughts of love. Such soul-love will be given expression in the physical, the same as all other thoughts produced. You may prefer to consider soul-love as belonging to the mental phase. The name you give it doesn't matter much, just so long as you understand that it is of separate and distinct origin. You may question the difference between soul-love and spiritual-love; therefore, we shall try to make that distinction a little clearer. Soul-love is under the direction of the soul-intelligence. Spiritual-love is under the direc-

191

tion of the life-spirit, the inner-consciousness.

"A parent may have a spiritual love for a child and carefully nurture it into manhood. The young man may commit a hideous crime and be condemned by society; but does the parent cease to love its child? No, the spiritual love remains constant. It is the soul-love that changes, for the intelligence of the parent causes him to distrust the child and despise the thing it has done. You see, there is quite a difference between soul-love and spiritual-love. One is governed by human intelligence while the other is governed by the inner-consciousness and is of an emotional origin. We may love our neighbors, yet detest the things they are doing.

"In dealing with the love-urge of the inner-consciousness, we are dealing with a basic emotion. It is the strongest of all human emotions, yet it is subject to the intelligent direction of the soul. That is, so long as the soul controls the process of mind. Remember, you cannot think of two things at one and the same time. The reason for that is that there is but one brain through which to produce thought. If your soul is directing your thought production, it can produce thoughts of hatred and disgust; but, should it release the control of the process of mind for one instant, the inner-consciousness may take over and produce thoughts of love. Do you now understand why you have at times acted contrary to your own best judgment?"

Reviewing the philosophy in, "Thoughtsmanship in Love and Marriage," Dr. Shaklee says:

"The best part of the whole thing is, IT WORKS ... Creative thought produced by the soul and given expression by the inner-consciousness is irresistible. I have invented nothing new. I am just presenting an old truth. Everyone wants to be happy in the present; but many allow their

192

thoughts of the past and of the future to ruin their enjoyment of the present."

He then cites the example of a woman mired in her past, with an unusually poverty-governed childhood. "Fear of poverty in the future has always filled my mind," says the woman. The distressing thoughts of the past and fear-thoughts of the future have crowded out all thoughts of happiness for this woman's present.

"Cultivate a change in your habit of thoughts," advises Dr. Shaklee. "Thought changes things."

"The importance of charity," says Dr. Shaklee, "is greatly misconstrued. Because charity is believed to be synonymous with love it is often not considered an attribute of love. Few people heed the warning that charity begins at home, and confine their charitable acts to institutional contributions." These acts, Dr. Shaklee feels, are done for ego satisfaction and do not represent the true giving of time or the sacrifice of pleasure. "Do you ever think of being charitable to those in your own home?" he asks. "Too many wives and husbands look upon the sacrifices of their companion as a matter of course. 'We're married now, so why shouldn't he give up a little time for me? I have to give up a lot of my time for him.'"

In marriage one assumes certain obligations, Dr. Shaklee concedes, but that doesn't lessen the desire for appreciation.

"Charity must not be given with the expectation of a return in kind, but it is natural to expect appreciation. We must consider charity as concomitant to love, and love seldom lives long without some reciprocation. Kindness seems to be patterned after the Law of Cohesion, for that is what binds us together."

In "Thoughtsmanship in Love and Marriage," Forrest tackles many of the demons of relating, such as anger, hatred and jealousy.

"Anger," says Forrest, "is a show of weakness. An angry person tries to make up with bluff and bluster what he lacks in the power of reason."

"Anger never overcomes anger in another."

"Never hate anyone," advises Forrest, "you may hate the things he does; but you should never hate the person. Hating what he does helps to prevent you from doing the same thing; but hating the person is quite likely to cause you to do unto him, what he has done unto you. He may then attempt to pay you in like coin and then the vicious cycle is formed."

"Hatred," says Forrest, "is soul madness." Forrest observes in this work that "oversensitivity is not a virtue but a fault. And it is a fault caused by over-developed self-pride. It is, in fact, no longer pride but vanity."

"And jealousy," Forrest maintains, "is the taskmaster who pays the bitterest wages . . ."

He further conjectures that, "if there is a Hell, the experiences of a jealous person are equal to the most horrible hell punishments ever conjured by the mind of man."

"Jealousy is the ultimate expression of self-love." Says Forrest, the ever practical sage, "How can you give your love to another when you are giving it to yourself?"

In this book, Forrest makes clear that there are no panaceas, and however sound, the best philosophy *cannot* help those who aren't willing to accept guidance. "Facts are where you find them and if future happiness is to be gained, we must acknowledge them".

Forrest's down-to-earth counselling, specifically to the bride, can be found in the following excerpts.

". . . Marital happiness is neither within, nor without—it is the blending of two individualities . . . dependent largely upon one's ability to be satisfied with the other . . . Happiness depends not so much on the nature of the events coming into your life but on how you meet those events . . ."

On the subject of affairs with others previous to the marriage, Forrest cautions the young bride. "Fears in any form will render you incapable of producing logical throught. True or false, there is nothing to be gained by pondering such a subject. Were he to ask you that question, would you feel a glow of pleasure? Would you give him a truthful answer, or would you feel distressed over his lack of confidence? Never, never allude to such a thing."

While in this work, Forrest holds that marriage consists of far more than sex; his ideas, expressed nearly thirty years ago on the matter, have the ring of today's most celebrated counselors.

"I wish to speak plainly but in no way do I want this message to suggest overemphasis on sex. Not that I, for one moment, subscribe to the old prudish idea that sex information should be discovered by mere chance. I believe that the sex life of any married couple is the greatest contributing factor to their happiness; that ignorance of the subject constitutes one of the main causes of divorce; that withholding sex information from our children makes parents a party to the crime that may, at some later date be committed . . ."

On trying to change a husband, Forrest advises, "Don't ruin your honeymoon by attempting to *Don't* your husband into becoming the kind of person You think he ought to be . . . if you must bring about a change in your companion, make that change in yourself . . . If you have developed the habit of fault-finding, start now replacing it with the habit of *praise*-finding . . ."

Forrest discusses Creative power in his book "Thoughtsmanship for Well-Being," and likens it to the power within the steam boiler of a locomotive. "Creative power," he says, "lies within you . . . It is of no value until given intelligent direction. The supply is unlimited. You may ration it out in small portions and acquire small measures of success, or you may open the throttle and drive on to your ultimate goal. Wrongly directed, it will cause your destruction for it is no respecter of persons . . . The responsibility is yours."

On the subject of fear he says:

"Perhaps there have been times when you were tormented by the consuming emotion of fear. Fear of

195

what? Is it the irrevocable past, the ever-fleeting present, or the impending future? Do you actually know why you are afraid? My experience, as counselor to thousands of fearful men and women, has revealed the fact that fear is usually grounded upon ignorance of the truth. We fear that which we fail to understand. If then, we fear our own past, present or future, it would appear that understanding should begin with ourselves. 'Man, know thyself.' Search for the good that is within you.

"I have been called upon to analyze the lives of many persons who actually hated themselves. Such hatred is always engendered by self-fear, for all hatred is based upon fear. We hate a certain person or thing, because we fear the effect that person or thing may have upon our well-being. To the student of thoughtsmanship there are no grounds for fear; thus, hatred is replaced by love; love of self as well as others. What a welcome change will take place in your life, once you have learned to conquer fear. *You can, if you think you can.*"

A clue to Forrest Shaklee's independent thinking can be gleaned by these statements in the same book:

"The trouble with most folk is that they emulate the humble sheep. They just follow the leader, thus taking the course of least resistance. Not knowing where they are being led, their lives are filled with indecision. The leader is usually looking out for no one but himself. To make sure that his followers serve his own selfish interests, he places artificial limits upon them. And, to make sure they stay within those limits, he instills them with fear of everything beyond that restricted sphere. That is true of all the selfish "isms" that have been inflicted upon the human race."

196

In this section, Forrest relates how for many years he, like other sheep-people, confined his thoughts to channels prescribed by leaders so filled with fear themselves that they were incompetent of leadership. "Yet," he says, "I was allowing them to determine my limits . . ."

"Has anyone placed limitations on your life?" he asks. "Are you hesitant to strike out on a new venture? . . . You are an individual. You must think as an individual, not as a collective flock of sheep. Never 'follow the leader' simply because he states a truth. Many so-called leaders possess only half a truth, yet attract a huge following. I would not speak discouragingly concerning anyone who is trying to lead others into a better understanding of self, but 'one button doesn't make a pair of pants,' even though that button may be a materially important part of the garment. Retain your individuality. Strive to ascertain the whole truth; then determine judiciously the use you should make of it."

"Thoughtsmanship for the Salesman," is more directly concerned with sound advice to those wishing to follow a sales career. Like his other books, Forrest's philosophy is interspersed with case histories told in the familiar folksy or parochial tone. However, in each of the examples that Forrest selects, the basic elements of common sense persist.

He tells us in "Thoughtsmanship for the Salesman" that, by recognizing the inner-consciousness as an endowment of the Creative Spirit, we can realize it as the motivating power of life. "It will carry out your thought orders. It is the greatest advertising and sales agency on earth. Your very thought is advertised and sold on the open market. How much you are worth on that market depends on the value of your thoughts. What value does the world place on you? *What you think you look; what you think you do; what you think you are.*"

Forrest maintains that while your prospect may not be a mind reader, the affirmative thoughts that you telegraph will prove impossible to reject. He cites as an example the following story:

"A little old lady came to my office one day and told the secretary she wanted to see me. When asked if she had an appointment, she replied, "No, but he'll see me."

The secretary was adroitly efficient and adhered strictly to office rules, but what chance had such rules against the broadcasting of such positive thoughts? I, too, was affected by those thoughts, for I readily consented to the unexpected interview. As I sat waiting for the intruder to make her appearance, there was an unexplainable emotion building up within me. In a moment the door opened and my caller was ushered in. Who was she? Who was this person whose thoughts had upset the routine of that well-organized office force and had aroused an emotional response in my inner-consciousness? My mother. She had planned that surprise, and had travelled two thousand miles for that very moment. Her thoughts had sold me on that visit, long before I knew who the creator of those thoughts was. Our thoughts do precede us in a sales interview. Do you wonder at the reception you sometimes receive?"

Martha Jane Shaklee had indeed travelled all the way from Iowa to Los Angeles. There she had taken a train to San Francisco, a bus over the bridge to Oakland and finally a taxi to Forrest's office. Certainly a lady of that indomitable spirit was not going to be thwarted in her purpose.

Shortly after Forrest had published the books on "Thoughtsmanship," Martha Jane died peacefully in Iowa. Another, and seemingly final page of Forrest's past, was closed. But, Dorothy was there to console him. With her sprightly gaiety and yet profound concern for others, Forrest was again reminded of how alike she was to his mother.

Chapter XXII

BY THE mid-nineteen fifties, Forrest's lectures had aroused enough interest that he followed them up with weekly radio talks. These were aired on KGO radio in San Francisco, and on station KWBR on Telegraph Avenue, in Oakland. There was, at that time, the barest glimmer of interest in ecology; pollution was not, as yet, a household word. But, Forrest repeatedly warned against the pillage of natural resources; repeatedly advised a sane and sensible regimen of nutrition. To meet the response from his lectures and programs, Forrest began to produce the products that had been the mainstay of his clinics. But, there was the question of distribution. The only avenue, available at that time, seemed to be health food stores, but these were considered faddish and did not enjoy the acceptance that they do today. And even with such outlets, the matter of controlling the length of time that the products remained on the shelves in the health food stores was of concern.

The few health food store owners that Forrest knew personally, simply could not provide the turnover to assure freshness. Under those circumstances, Forrest was not prepared to put his name on the products. So, the publicity that he was gaining did not as yet serve any practical purpose.

From the days of Casimir Funk and his early *vitamines,* the field of nutrition had grown only gradually. Although the ancients, among them Hippocrates, the Father of Medicine, had recommended the eating of animal livers against night blindness, and the bark and leaves of a type of spruce for the prevention of scurvy had been used successfully in the sixteenth century, acceptance in scientific circles of the need for nutritional supplements was won virtually by degrees.

By the nineteen-forties the attitude had almost imperceptibly shifted from disease-preventing to health-maintaining. A scientific tone was more evident in the research that was to continue until the present day.

Since this whole area was a subject of vital importance to him, Forrest studied each new development with interest. In the early nineteen-fifties, the nutritional element that preoccupied him almost exclusively, was that of protein. In 1838, a Dutch chemist by the name of Mulder, coined the term protein, meaning "to take first place." In her book, INTRODUCTORY NUTRITION,[1] Dr. Helen Guthrie says: "Although it is now difficult to maintain that protein is more important than other nutrients, it is unlikely that Mulder had any conception of the extremely important roles this group of compounds plays in the body or of the number and complexity of the protein components of the body and of food. We now have evidence that protein is a constituent of every living cell." Interest in protein was high in the beginning of the century, but waned with the discovery of vitamins between the two world wars.

A protein deficiency disease Kwashiorkor, that affected a great portion of the world's population, improved testing measures, and the acknowledgement that blood and plasma transfusions could save lives, were factors that revived the interest in protein again.

Forrest began to experiment with protein compounds. Now, more than ever, Forrest was convinced that the time was precisely right for the introduction of nutritional supplements tailored as closely to nature as possible. And, his incentive to succeed in this venture was doubly intensified since meeting Dorothy. He had promised himself that he would only ask her to marry him when he could provide for her in a truly worthy manner. He felt that a man with an ideal unfulfilled, was an unfulfilled man.

So, he met with his sons to discuss various means of making the Shaklee products available on a wide distribution basis. Most importantly, the method of distribution must include as much personal contact with the consumer as possible. The people who sold Shaklee products would have to be exposed, not only to the products, but to the philosophy behind them.

By now, Forrest, Jr.'s accounting business was growing steadily. He was married to the former Glenda Crecelius, a young woman of engaging friendliness and a dazzling smile. They had a son, Clifford.

Making his mark in the insurance field, Lee too, married. Fate, in storybook style, had thrown Lee and an ethereal blonde, Claire Ahern, together one night on the dance floor of the El Patio Ballroom in San Francisco. A mutual love of dancing (which persists to this day) led to romance and marriage. Their son was named Richard.

Both young men had worked their ways up the rungs of business. Each had amassed a respectable degree of success, and each had developed areas of business acumen that complemented the other. Doctor Shaklee and his sons conferred for months, working late into the night, for an innovative distribution and sales plan. When the skeleton of what was to become the Shaklee organization was drafted, Doctor Shaklee presented the format to his bankers and accountants. Without exception, they thought he had taken leave of his senses. They could not foresee a people-business, based on good nutrition. They thought that the premise of The Golden Rule as a policy was naive—and they certainly could not foresee success.

But, Forrest, Jr. and Lee saw all these things positively, and they would not deny their vision. They were prepared to risk their hard-earned security and pitch in their lots with their father. Fired up by what they felt was an extraordinary opportunity, they were quick to act on it.

In his sumptuous Victorian-styled office, Lee describes his initial reaction as exactly the spirit of "gung-ho," that moved him to enlist in the war.

"Of course we were 'gung-ho,'" says Lee, "because my father, my brother and I certainly knew where we were going. After all, insurance is person-to-person on a very businesslike level, and so is accounting. In fact, when a doctor sits across his desk, he is one-on-one with his patients.

"And, don't forget, in addition to this business experience, my brother and I had a lifetime exposure to proper nutrition.

"Those formulas were part of our childhood, not only in our own diets, but in the fact that when they were in powdered form, we used to sit after school and help with packaging them. We learned about the products from a very grass-roots level."

Forrest, Jr., recalls that he was equally enthusiastic. Reminiscing in his functionally tailored office, Forrest also emphasizes the fact that he and his brother had grown up in a nutrition-conscious environment.

"We knew firsthand of its value to the average person. In person-to-person selling, we felt we could get across the idea that with a quality product there was no way they would not plain feel better, look better and have a greater sense of well-being. So, when Dad said that he had developed some products which he felt worthy of putting the Shaklee name on—well, the challenge to formulate something from the ground up was exciting."

Person-to-person selling was the keystone around which the Shaklee organization was built. At the outset, the Shaklees were agreed that the business would be based on direct-to-consumer selling of product.

When the salesperson had accrued a certain sales volume, he would rise in rank, and as he brought new people into his sales organization, he would receive overrides on their sales. Joining a Shaklee sales group would never depend on a mandatory purchase of product. To this day, the new Distributor need only buy the new Distributor Kit at a nominal sum, to start a business with excellent possibilities.

From Dr. Shaklee's viewpoint, the business had to comply with the basic tenet of cooperation with nature. Of that beginning in 1956, where, at last, he and his two sons were to make a reality of this lifelong pursuit, Dr. Shaklee says, "Man has been endowed with a natural instinct, the same as other animals, except that all other animals are more susceptible to the demands of Nature than is man. Man knows too much that is not true, and he tries to assert his will over the Laws of Nature. Of course, in such instances, he gets his fingers burned. Nature has a plan; if you fit it you win. Buck it and you lose.

"So in organizing the original Shaklee Products Company, we attempted to organize this whole setup in harmony with Nature in hopes that those who came later would realize the necessity of perpetuating that rule of Nature in the operation of the company."

From this starting point of an inspired idea, the groundwork began. Since he now considered protein to be the most important food of man and since lecithin too, was found in the framework of all cells, Forrest had developed a product which contained some of both. The name given this product was Pro-Lecin. It would be the vanguard of the many nutritional supplements and foods that Forrest had used with excellent results over the years in his practice.

Space requirements, packaging and labeling were the next factors to be taken into account. Certainly there had to be a Sales Plan. This was designed to allow the Distributor the maximum return on his sales effort. The cost of production was carefully analyzed and the wholesale price established.

The "triumvirate" was formed, with Dr. Shaklee providing the technical expertise, and equally important, his lifelong principles. Forrest, Jr. provided his organizational and business management skills, while Lee applied his talent for salesmanship and promotion in marketing. Given these three essentials for business operation, the remaining factor was salespeople. The unique nature of direct sales, coupled with the sincere belief required in the Golden Rule principles, demanded very specific types of salespeople.

The first Shaklee Products office was established on 14th

Street in Oakland, California. This office consisted of a desk and part of a storage room. Office duties were handled by one woman, an excellent stenographer who also performed numerous other tasks. Lee recalls that it was not very efficiently laid out, but he remembers that there was a very large filing cabinet in which to keep the sales records of their hoped-for sales group.

Their first sales meeting was held in the home of a couple who were experienced in personal selling. There were six prospective salesmen who attended that meeting. Dr. Shaklee spoke of the opportunities in Shaklee. Of the six in attendance, five signed Distributor Applications, and the sixth called at the office the next day and signed his application. They had just one product to sell: Pro-Lecin.

Of this initial recruiting, Forrest, Jr. says, "for some time we operated just like a new Distributor would today; sponsor a Distributor and then help him sponsor others. Basically, we were never interested in sponsoring a large group of people under the company. We were interested in building sales groups. Obviously, there had to be a starting point. We helped new members build their groups because we were more interested in their training their new people than we were in adding greater numbers."

While Dr. Shaklee was concerned with the overall program, Forrest, Jr. and Lee assisted in sales, taking and filling orders, even in the delivery and distribution of products. An early employee recalls that, "Lee, Forrest, Jr., and Doctor respected one another's areas of responsibility. If anyone asked Doctor about the Sales Plan, bonuses or orders, he quickly told the inquirer, 'You'll have to check with my boys about that, I don't get into their work. They know their business a lot better than I.' " About the Shaklee sons, that old timer remembers: "Forrest, Jr. worked every waking moment at making the business thrive. He kept in personal touch with every account over and above his dedication to keeping product orders and bonuses running at maximum efficiency.

"Lee was the Sales Voice of Shaklee, keeping a constant watch on the administration of the sales organization. Lee was the articulate speaker who *sold* his ideas and helped the company grow. 'You have to keep the hoop rolling,' Lee would say."

The hoop certainly rolled. The orders grew, as did the sales force, with a gradual but solid momentum. Such growth required a move to larger quarters. These were acquired at 1610 Harrison Street and later to larger quarters at 12th and Harrison, in Oakland, California.

With wry humor, Lee recalls the basement of that office: "The stairway leading down to that basement was very steep and you had to be very careful that you didn't break your neck. We all referred to it as the dungeon." Dungeon notwithstanding, the business was still growing.

Short-handed, with only one additional woman to take phone orders, the three Shaklees fulfilled every function required to market and sell their products. This included developing promotional material. Lee relates how the Gestetner machine was in the dungeon, ready to crank out product brochures, meeting announcements and LSP-O's, as the first price lists were called.

If Shaklee is a people-to-people business, the sales force depends for its strength, on the unity of couples. It was usually the wife who signed up as a Distributor, often with no more than the idea of making a small supplementary income. Selling Shaklee, she soon found, was an area in which women could shine with unmatched brilliance. A standard bit of Shaklee folklore, is the parable of the husband who takes a tolerantly amused view of his wife's "little" venture. Soon he begins to be impressed by the sheer volume of her sales. And, finally, when her income surpasses his, he decides the time has come to step in and show her how to run a business.

A case in point, is that of one of Shaklee's leading Master Coordinators. The husband, a Minneapolis policeman, fell into the classic role of the disinterested, but not discouraging husband. Disinterest changed to amazement and then awe, when single-handedly, his wife surpassed his salary and then the incomes of his Police Chief, the Mayor, and finally the Governor. The wives are quick to welcome their husbands into Shaklee, and the husbands are the first to credit their wives perspicacity. The combined efforts of each have proven dynamic.

That the distaff of any team in Shaklee is at the very least a tremendous catalyst, was demonstrated by the wives of Dr. Shaklee, Forrest, Jr., and Lee. While their husbands had been responsible for launching the business, Dorothy, Glenda and Claire were principle motivators and pacesetters for the women who joined the company.

At the meetings which eventually grew into Conventions, these women with their natural vibrancy, provided enormous impetus. Unfailingly warm and vivacious, Dorothy, as the doyenne of the three, and wife of Dr. Shaklee, is revered by the field force. Referring to the woman who worked by his side from the beginning of this ultimate adventure, Dr. Shaklee says, "There is only one Dorothy, My Dorothy." This adoration is echoed by the sales force, who refer to her as "Our Dorothy."

Dorothy Shaklee has a little-girl ingenuousness that makes one think of a grown-up Princess Dorothy of Oz. Combined with a natural spontaneity and great diplomacy, is an extraordinary memory for names. No one quite has Dorothy's gift for putting a person at ease. Like her husband, Dorothy's accessability is a natural part of her—she genuinely cares about multitudes of people. With a sovereign's unerring instinct for style, she never overdresses, and has a vital sense of line and color to befit the occasion.

From her grandparents, who were merchants of fine bone china, Dorothy inherited a taste for collecting rare porcelain. Among her more prized pieces are some fine examples of Staffordshire, and Royal Doulton.

It must be said that each of the Shaklee wives is an original. Glenda, Forrest, Jr.'s wife, is a "hail fellow, well met" personality. Fun loving and direct, Glenda is a perfect match for Forrest, Jr. With a kind of Eva Tanguay nonchalance about style, Glenda is as likely to emerge in elegant brocades as to toss a mink coat over blouse and slacks. Unaffected and genuinely interested in people, Glenda will hold forth in groups keeping the merriment alive with her brand of irreverent humor. Sparkling eyes and a radiant smile enhance Glenda's prettiness. Glenda's talents include gardening, a fine eye for paintings and she enjoys no small reputation as a gourmet cook.

Elegance for its own sake is sometimes static, but not so when applied to Claire Shaklee, who can best be described as elegant with great verve. Whether in a pantsuit, flowing print, or a stiletto sheath of sequins, Claire always manages a certain panache. Trim, blonde and with a honeygrain voice reminiscent of actress Jean Arthur, Claire's is the first-lady type of graciousness. While both she and Lee will readily get into the spirit of a Shaklee fun occasion, both also have definite presence.

Those incipient years of the Shaklee business are full of memories for Dorothy, Glenda and Claire, who assisted, lending their moral support, and then in a more tangible way, by helping with the increasing office work.

Dorothy recalls hours spent just looking for useable furniture for the first Shaklee office at 1610 Harrison Street, carefully making selections that were practical and durable. Sales Leaders of those early days, remember with some nostalgia, when a Shaklee meeting was small enough that it could boast in its programs, of not just one Shaklee, but of the whole family.

Glenda is remembered affectionately for her cheerful attendance with Forrest, Jr., at meetings held in Los Angeles for a grand total of seven *possible* sales people.

For Glenda, the visits later included meetings in Stockton, Fresno and Bakersfield. "We just did it," Glenda laughs. "After all this was to be *our* Shaklee family—and they were."

Claire's assistance to Lee was twofold. Not only did she support her husband at meetings, but steadfastly handled all his correspondence and the volumes of paperwork that crossed his desk.

In a recent interview, Claire was quoted as saying, "I did not abandon my typewriter until the arrival of my daughter Laura." And, although Laura was followed by daughters Sandra and Karen, Claire, like Dorothy and Glenda, still continued her contacts with the people who grew into the immense Shaklee family field force.

By today's standards of super-produced conventions, early meetings were simple and basic. Groups then were small, products few, but enthusiasm was at a pitch. Soon after the Shaklee Products Company was launched, Dorothy and Doctor Shaklee decided to give a Christmas party for their sales people. The location was at the 12th and Harrison offices in Oakland. Dorothy and Doctor Shaklee cooked the turkey; Dorothy's mother baked a ham and made real English plum pudding and Christmas cake, for the dessert. This was the first Shaklee Celebration for their sixty or so sales people.

The Shaklees had stayed up all night preparing for the feast. Dorothy had set the table with her finest linen and sterling, and everyone seemed to be having an enjoyable time.

Dorothy noticed that among the guests was someone that she had no recollection of meeting. Nor, it appeared, had anyone else in the group brought the lady. Still the stranger went on sampling everything and returning for second and third helpings. Finally, Dorothy noticed that the woman was putting food into a brown paper bag. Unable to contain her curiosity, Dorothy went over to the lady and very tactfully asked who had brought her.

"Oh, nobody," the woman replied. "I just happened to be walking by and saw a party going on. And listen, I want you to know this food is *excellent*."

Caught between the humor of the situation and a

determination to make her generosity pay off, Dorothy told the woman about Shaklee products, suggested that she take some cards and recommend the products to her friends.

"And," Dorothy adds, "you know, we actually got a couple of sales people from her."

With his dream beginning to be realized, Forrest now felt free to ask Dorothy to marry him. By now, both Doctor Shaklee and Dorothy had amassed so many friends, it seemed wisest to make this very personal committment a private one as well.

On August 8th, 1957, Forrest and Dorothy took their vows in a moonlight ceremony, on the shores of Lake Tahoe. Forrest remembers that during the ceremony, the waters lapped to the edge of the beach getting his shoes thoroughly wet. In typically Dr. Shaklee humor, he says, "in all the time that I had known My Dorothy, that was the only moment that I got cold feet."

Chapter XXIII

FORREST SHAKLEE has often said, "nobody does it alone." Specifically, he is referring to the multi-million dollar Shaklee empire that began as a vision in 1915, with his first bottle of vitalized minerals. "Besides a dictate from nature to do what I *had* to, I have had tremendous help—" he credits his sons for seizing upon that vision and working hard to help attain it; he heaps praise upon the Distributor in the field who carried the torch and lit the way for others to follow.

Typically, Forrest seeks no personal credit. "We have given our people nothing," he says, "except the opportunity to succeed. Those who really wanted to and could, did. It's as simple as that."

The field force began as a few hardy souls, who believed in the products, used them personally and talked them up to others. These dedicated pioneers soon coined the phrase, "Don't just tell it to tell it, but tell it to sell it."

Those who began as Distributors and rapidly attained the sales rank of Supervisor, were initially from California. Later, Sales Leaders were to burgeon from every state. As the numbers of sales people grew, it became clear to the Shaklees that by-laws were required and desirable for this business, and so, the tract called Privileges and Responsibilities (P&R) was written. As Lee Shaklee explains it, "It is impossible to legislate morality. But what the P&R expresses is simply that we, the company, are going to follow the Golden Rule. And, because we do, we now have a right to demand that you do. And, if you don't believe it, make us prove it . . ."

In addition to these sales force by-laws, some years later a Supervisor's Handbook provided details for the management of that position. And, early in the business the Shaklee father and sons realized that higher ranks with greater

210

rewards for effort were required. A study was made of the many direct sales plans; workable ideas were gained from such plans and became the building blocks of the now successful Shaklee Sales Plan. Lee, being head of the Sales Organization, was authorized to make such additions, as the level of Assistant Supervisor and later the higher rank of Coordinator. The bonus structure was changed to percentages which remained in effect until January 1976.

The company that had begun with first one, and then five Distributors in 1956 had come a long way, and was to continue its dramatic upward climb. In 1958, there were 1,000 Distributors in the field sales force. By 1962, sales were equal to almost all the previous years combined. And, in that year, Shaklee began expanding its facilities in Hayward. The office at 2035 National Avenue opened its doors. Dr. Shaklee and his sons reasoned that the time had come to incorporate. It was at this time, that Forrest, Jr. and Glenda's son, Cliff, joined the company.

A major in accounting and architectural drafting at Oakland City College, Cliff found his metier in computer programming. It was he who set up the original payroll and bonus system which, at the time, computer experts lauded as highly sophisticated, and which, with minor modifications is still in use at Shaklee.

Lee and Claire's son, Richard (Rick), very shortly made himself indispensable in the promotional aspects of the company, relieving his father of some of that burden. Doctor Shaklee and his two sons are each endowed with exceptionally fine speaking voices, and they were now able to exert their individual personalities in auditoriums crowded with people eager to hear them.

While of a more folksy personality than either his father or brother, Forrest, Jr. is nonetheless dynamic. What he projects is the classic, "call a spade a spade" approach. The field force may cringe slightly at the directness of his message, but approval is strongly registered by the enthusiastic applause.

Lee, on the other hand, while equally direct, manages an

211

executive aura. His firepower is charismatic, but his presence demands accountability. And, if William Jennings Bryan was the Peerless Leader to those who thronged the Chautauquas, no less was Dr. Shaklee to the 150 Supervisors at the Jack Tar Hotel in San Francisco. The occasion was the first National Supervisors Convention. The theme of the Convention was, "A Touch of Luxury,"—the year was 1964.

The next year's convention was dedicated to the fiftieth anniversary of Dr. Shaklee's first product, Vitalized Minerals. The theme of that convention was "The Golden Anniversary," and it was held at the San Francisco Hilton Hotel.

By now the line of nutritional supplements had been expanded to include Herb-lax, Vita-Lea (the original Vitalized Minerals now in tablet form), Liqui-Lea, a liquid vitamin, and later, Instant Protein. New lines of cleaners, cosmetics and personal care items were being added. The household cleaners were unique in that they were perhaps the first to address themselves to the needs of ecology. Nearly all of these products are biodegradable and non-polluting.

Dr. Shaklee's intuition for the timing of certain key products is best illustrated by the following anecdote:

A California Supervisor telephoned Dr. Shaklee from Southern California to inform him that inroads were being made on his group by someone who had gone East and returned with a concentrated cleaning fluid; the product was attracting many of his Distributors. He explained the urgency of the situation and asked if it were possible for Shaklee to produce a similar product. Dr. Shaklee replied, "Well, I'll send down some samples." Whereupon the Supervisor asked, "When will you have them ready?" Forrest inquired, "Would tomorrow morning be soon enough?"

That night, with Dorothy's help, two small vials of clear blue liquid were placed on the Greyhound Bus, in Oakland.

In less than forty-eight hours, the Sales Leader had received the two small vials of clear blue liquid. There were no instructions and no details, but at a meeting, the Shaklee product was tested against the competitive product in a variety of applications. It was once again a matter of, "Don't just tell it to tell it, but tell it to sell it," and the tiny samples performed with such eloquence that there was no more question of Distributors straying to an outside line.

The product was Basic-H, and sales of this multipurpose cleaning concentrate were so dramatic that they *marked the turning point* in Shaklee's sales history. But, how this product was discovered by Dr. Shaklee may give a clue to his inventiveness.

One night while he was engaged in processing a certain oil, the gears of the machine suddenly became crossmeshed, breaking the gears, and spilling some of the oil. In examining them, Dr. Shaklee found his hands coated with an oily substance. He discovered that upon wiping his hands with a paper towel, he removed all the grime caused by touching the broken gear, leaving his hands perfectly clean. Without any specific purpose in mind at that point, he recorded the formula of the substance for future possible use. Subsequent tests showed that the substance was biodegradable and in harmony with Dr. Shaklee's concerns for nature. Thus, when the crisis occured, Dr. Shaklee's earlier thought, committed to action, became the basis of one of the most popular products in the Shaklee line.

Two days later, Forrest received another phone call from the Sales Leader who excitedly described the results of their tests of the cleaner. "But what are you going to call it?" asked the Sales Leader. "Well," replied Forrest, "it's a good hand cleaner and it is made from basic oils. Why not call it, BASIC-H."

The growth of business which originated from sales in the field was reflected in the advances made by the Shaklee father and sons.

In 1965, 13,000 industrious Distributors created enough sales to warrant the company doubling the original 10,000 square footage of the plant in Hayward. And, by 1969, new field titles of eminence were devised to honor those with outstanding records of sales and sponsorship.

These new titles were designated as Key and Master Coordinators. To become a Key Coordinator, a Supervisor was required to develop nine first level Supervisors. The rank of Master Coordinator required development of fifteen first level Supervisors. In August of 1969, three Supervisor teams and one single Supervisor became Shaklee's first Keys. And, in December, one of those couples became the first Master Coordinator team in Shaklee.

The following year, 1970, saw an increase of the Hayward production area to 70,000 square feet. This expansion included more office, warehousing and computer programming space. Five million pounds of product were being shipped and there were now over 50,000 Distributors. At the end of that year, the first Shaklee warehouse outside of Hayward opened its doors in Edina, Minnesota.

In 1972, twelve Master Coordinators presided at a Convention of over 2,000 Sales Leaders, By the following March, the Shaklee Corporation had become a publicly-owned company, so that the field force who had made it all possible could share in its growth. 1973 was another record year of sales, and as a tribute to their success, the National Coordinators Convention was held in Hawaii—indeed Partners in Progress. With a continuing upward spiral in field growth, the year's end showed 8,300 Assistant Supervisors, 2,300 Supervisors and 250 Coordinators. Shaklee Corporate Headquarters moved to the Shaklee Towers on the Emeryville shores of San Francisco Bay.

In the early nineteen-seventies, the surging success of their business made Dr. Shaklee, Forrest, Jr., and Lee, aware that if they were not to spread themselves to the point of diminishing value, they must hire strong support management. This was a difficult process, made doubly intricate by the need for men with proven records in executive management, as well as men who had a receptivity to the philosophy that had launched the business. With careful searching and sifting this was accomplished, and in March of 1973, Shaklee became a public corporation.

The act of becoming a public corporation was a move that occupied as much time, energy and concern as the Shaklee father and sons had spent in originating the Company. The rationale for finally doing so is expressed by each of the founders. Says Dr. Shaklee:

"I frankly welcomed the idea of having Shaklee stock listed on the open market for everyone to purchase and participate in. I believed not only in the dollars and cents they might get out of their investment; that's the least part of it as far as I'm concerned—but if a person has become financially interested in a business, he is more likely to absorb some of its philosophy. And, it's the schooling that *he* gets which does us the most good. The more people who realize the significance of the Shaklee Philosophy, the effect it has on humanity and particularly the effect it has on the thousands upon thousands of Shaklee Distributors who are carrying that philosophy in the homes of so many folks, the more likely it's going to have an effect on the commercial world."

Lee Shaklee takes a broad-scope view:

"Going public was a move to accomplish a wide variety of things. The people in the field cannot help but benefit from corporate flexibility. A public company is able to establish connections with outside business interests, such as banks, and suppliers which are essential to the operations of a business of this size. All of this enhances our ability to do a better job. It means being better known, moving once again into the mode of practicing what we preach and the idea of having the self-confidence to open our doors. Most importantly, it gives the sales force the opportunity if they choose, to become part of the corporation."

And, with his inimitable matter-of-factness, Forrest, Jr. adds:

> "I believe there are only three reasons why a company goes public. One: In order to bail out, which we had no intention of doing. Two: Increased cash, which we don't really need. Or three: So that there could be an equitable sharing of the company through the purchase of stock. And, this last was our motivating factor. To give everyone a chance to participate in the future, particularly the guy out there in the field."

In tandem with the independent sales field family, the Shaklee Corporation family began to harness its growth, and in 1974 there were strategically-located Regional Distribution Centers, and more planned. A uniform national delivered pricing and a single Order Processing Center helped to streamline service to the field. Shaklee, now a household word in the entire United States, began to spread to European markets, and that was the year that, with separate marketing plans and independent manufacturing facilities, Shaklee became international. And, as if foretelling the banner year ahead, a jubilant National Convention was held in San Juan, Puerto Rico in January 1975.

From the inspired thought of a man and his two sons, a modest beginning of five Distributors and a purchase volume of $100,000, the Shaklee Corporation had grown to the respected and impressive corporation whose sales growth exceeded $100,000,000 in 1975. It has become, to the over 5,000 Sales Leaders and thousands of Shaklee Distributors, no less than a movement.

The United States Bicentennial in 1976 marked as well,

Shaklee's twentieth anniversary as a company. The analogy between the two anniversaries was made valid by the fact that both began with no more than a vision from which evolved the best attributes of what is commonly called the American Dream—personal freedom, independence of choice and an opportunity to scale the heights. The Shaklee slogan for 1976 was, "Shaklee 20 years of Opportunity—America 200 years of Freedom".

This theme was vividly celebrated in a convention held at the San Francisco Civic Auditorium—with over 2,000 Supervisors in attendance. At the end, a candlelit ceremony was enacted with an actor playing Benjamin Franklin lighting the first candle, which he passed to Dr. Shaklee, who then lit the candle of each executive, who in turn lit the candle of others, and as each one in the Auditorium lit the candle of his neighbor, the room glowed with the flames of 2,000 candles.

Coordinators met for their Convention in Acapulco where new products and an anniversary issue commemorating Shaklees growth were introduced.

And, in 1976, sales reached nearly $170,000,000.

International Operations have been restructured to emphasize growth potential in England, Canada, and Japan. Five regional distribution centers now handle the volume of domestic product flow, and are located in Hayward, California, Chicago, Illinois, Lyndhurst, New Jersey, Dallas, Texas and Atlanta, Georgia.

The Board of Directors includes the two co-founders, Forrest, Jr. and Lee in a group of top flight executives. With widely diverse backgrounds, each is a luminary in his field.

While the Shaklees remain major stockholders and keep a vigilant eye on the course of company developments, they are now able for the first time in over twenty years to enjoy other aspects of life.

Forrest, Jr. and Glenda are active in the special research in genetic problems, conducted by the Children's Hospital in San Francisco. They are as well, members of the Concern

217

Foundation, based in Los Angeles and contribute to its research. Over and above donations, they attend the seminars and lectures on cancer and genetic diseases.

To her wide repertoire of cooking, Glenda has now added Chinese cuisine and is learning the subtleties of Chinese gourmet cooking. With more time to spend in gardening, Glenda has developed a fine green thumb; her patio and house abound with exotic plants. A naturally fine eye for painting has led to collecting, and some major artists' works grace the walls of their home.

For the past twenty years, Forrest, Jr. has loaned his bass voice to the Eden-Hayward Chapter of Barber Shop Quartets. His group is called "The Sports." They have been Western U.S. District Champions three times and Northern California regional champions five times. In addition, Forrest, Jr., finds the time to be active with the Lions Club. Their son, Cliff, is handling special computer research programs.

Beyond being able to enjoy family life with their recently-wed son, Rick, and his bride, and to help chart the education of their daughters Laura, Sandie and Karen, Lee and Claire are imbued in cultural activities. They have made generous donations to both the Oakland Symphony and to the recently restored Paramount Theatre. Lee recalls that when his family finally settled in the Oakland area after that long journey from Florida to Oregon in the early thirties, he watched in awe, the opening of the Paramount Theatre. More leisure has now allowed Lee the time to devote to his ham radio operations, and to both Lee and Claire, their unquenchable enthusiasm for dancing. As often as not, after some gala function, the two will slip away like an eager pair of teenage contestants, and blissfully dance away the hours at a local dance hall.

Always a champion for women's equality, Lee maintains an age-old courtliness. Both he and Claire are strongly aware that equal rights for women requires that those women have qualifications equal to men. At present, their nineteen year old Laura is spending her sophomore year at a college in Switzerland.

Lee and Claire both contribute to, and take a keen interest in the Juniper branch of the Children's Hospital, as well as the San Antonio Youth Project. Another project to which Lee feels particularly close, is the Northern California DX Foundation, a radio operation which financially supports communications with foreign countries.

Gracious entertainment as part of gracious living is enjoyed by the Raleigh Shaklees. But, most of all, their contentment appears to be in each other.

Appointed Chairman Emeritus by Shaklee's Board of Directors in 1975, Dr. Shaklee uses his respite from the day to day chores to create new chores. In an "off limits" study in their Castro Valley home, Dr. Shaklee spends several hours each day expanding his philosophical premises and honing his existing ones. Notes for possible new formulations are jotted down.

Mindful of this need for privacy, Dorothy engages herself in household and humanitarian activities. Although she, herself, would never volunteer this information, a great portion of her time is spent in helping the less fortunate. Until recently, Dorothy would take the patients of a nursing home for long drives in her limousine. This thoughtfulness is not expressed in the sense of the chatelaine doing good works, but rather from a simple appreciation of her own better circumstances. Because of the possible consequences should any of the patients become ill on these outings, Dorothy was advised by the Director of the home to discontinue them. Undaunted, she now packs hampers of food and what she calls "necessary luxuries," which she takes with her on visits. Doctor and Dorothy contribute to numerous charities, about which they prefer to remain anonymous.

It is impossible to imagine anyone not being cheered by the ebullient Dorothy and her contagious joy, but Dr. Shaklee expresses the concern that she gives more of herself than she can physically spare. By his own report we know that

Dorothy never shirks even the slightest of Dr. Shaklee's comforts. Each day, when he emerges from his shower, his suit, with appropriate shirt, socks and shoes are carefully laid out for him. Freedom from the mandatory daily working stint has allowed Doctor and Dorothy to catch up on travel-sightseeing and visiting their many friends all over the world.

Gardening is another working pastime that they share, and Dr. Shaklee declares that "Dorothy makes a very good garden boss. We have a gardener who does the actual labor and she bosses both of us. She bosses me first, then I go out and take it out on the gardener." Both Doctor and Dorothy take pride in their roses. When they began their rose garden, they went to various flower shows to learn the newer hybrids. Though both enjoy flowers of all sorts, Dorothy has command of these while Doctor Shaklee specializes in shrubs.

The grounds in the senior Shaklee's home reflect their love of nature. In the front lawn is a small lake of 8,000 gallons, populated with many species of fish. Surrounding the lake is shrubbery planted by Dr. Shaklee, not in any formalized design, but in asymmetrical patterns, as they would have grown naturally.

Miniature mountains rise up from the lake, with waterfalls cascading over the peaks. Says Dr. Shaklee, "It's a source of inspiration to sit out there and contemplate the lake and the mountains with the rushing sound of the waterfalls. And soon . . . in my mind's eye, the scene becomes magnified and I am out in the real mountains . . ."

Asked what he feels is the one major characteristic most representative of his wife, Dr. Shaklee says without hesitation, "Not what she says, but the feeling I get from her presence. Just an innate source of communication." Asked the same question in relation to her husband, Dorothy replies, "His unselfishness and his honesty. Perhaps one of the first things I thought about when we met was, what a perfectly open, honest man he is . . ."

Much of Dr. Shaklee and Dorothy's time is spent in attending conventions—they are still the greatest draw at any meeting. The turnout for a Shaklee Convention at which he is speaking, sometimes exceeds 15,000 people.

To any two people less secure and genuinely humble than the senior Shaklee couple, the welcoming roar that emanates when they enter an auditorium, might have an ego-inflating effect. Dr. Shaklee's reaction to this illustrates his sense of balance: "I don't know what all the fuss is about. I appreciate the expressions of love but people shouldn't try to make a hero out of me. All I ever did was to listen to Nature and pass the word along."

Obviously, with such attendance, security is provided for Dr. Shaklee at conventions. Although he realizes the hazards of over-zealous well-wishers, who want to shake his hand and take his picture, Dr. Shaklee accepts the security measures grudgingly. "Since they've taken the trouble to come and hear me, I wish it were possible to greet each and every one personally."

Honors have been accrued along the way. In 1968, Dr. Shaklee was given a Special Recognition Award, by the California Secretary of State. While he appreciates these honors, Forrest Shaklee, Sr. tends to take them in stride. In fact, when the Shaklee Corporation was launched and he felt that he would never again return to practice, he was all for discarding the files of accumulated degrees and awards. It was only at Dorothy's gentle urging that he allowed them to be stored.

Like his sons, Dr. Shaklee maintains and uses his office at the Shaklee Towers in Emeryville. There in a suite with turf green carpeting and wood panelling, surroundings that reflect his need to be encompassed by a sense of nature, Dr. Shaklee discusses the phenomenon that grew into the Shaklee Corporation.

"I have lived my life by visualization," he says, "but what has been achieved by those great people in the field, is beyond even my vision."

Does Dr. Shaklee feel that the movement which he and his sons began twenty-one years ago has reached its zenith? A smile of pure mischief lights his face as he replies, "You ain't seen nothin' yet!"

About the Author

Georges Spunt is the author of three books, including an autobiography, A PLACE IN TIME. In the years since Mr. Spunt came from China and established his reputation as a writer in the United States, he has been a sales and sales promotion executive. It is this insight into both worlds—the creative and the pragmatic, which makes him keenly sensitive to the story of this philosopher-businessman.

FOOTNOTES

Foreword

1. Clarence Darrow, *The Story Of My Life,* Charles Scribner's Sons, copyright © 1932, Charles Scribner's Sons; renewal copyright © 1960, Mary D. Simonson, Jessie D. Lyon and Blanche Chase, p.1.

2. Roger Burlingame, *Henry Ford,* Alfred A. Knopf, A Borzoi Book, copyright © 1954, p. 7.

Chapter 1

1. Edwin Tunis, *Frontier Living,* Collins-World Publishers, Inc., copyright © 1961, p. 72.

2. Herbert Eaton, *The Overland Trail to California,* G.P. Putnam's Sons, copyright © 1974, p. 7.

3. *Ibid.,* p. 9.   6. *Ibid.,* p. 116.

4. Tunis, p. 116.   7. Eaton, p. 5.

5. *Ibid.,* p. 73.   8. Ibid., pp. 8-9.

9. Herb Hake, *Iowa Inside Out,* Iowa State University Press, copyright © 1968, p. 16.

10. Phil Stong, *Hawkeyes,* Harold Matson Company, Inc., copyright © 1940, 1968.

Chapter 2

1. Hake, pp. 8-15.   7. *Ibid.,* p. 79.

2. *Ibid.,* p. 27.   8. *Ibid.,* p. 52.

3. *Ibid.,* p. 37.   9. *Ibid.,* pp. 71-72.

4. *Ibid.,* pp. 39-40.   10. *Ibid.,* pp. 66-67.

5. *Ibid.,* pp. 50-51.   11. *Ibid.,* p. 56.

6. *Ibid.,* pp. 51-52.

Chapter 3

1. Mabel Owens Shaffer, *History of Carlisle and Vicinity,* Iowa State Historical Society, p. 72.

2. *Ibid.,* p. 74.

3. *Ibid.,* p. 78.

4. H.M. Pratt, *History of Ft. Dodge And Webster County, Iowa,* Pioneer Press, copyright © 1913, p. 116.

5. *Ibid.,* p. 116.   6. *Ibid.,* p. 173.

Chapter 4

1. Hake, pp. 135-138.

2. *Ibid.*, p. 140.
3. *Ibid.*, p. 170.

Chapter 5
1. Shaffer, p. 74.

Chapter 6
1 Bernarr Macfadden, *Encyclopedia of Physical Culture,* Bernarr
Macfadden Foundation, Inc., copyright © 1912, p. 4.
2. Public Domain

Chapter 7
1. Russell Lord, *The Wallaces Of Iowa,* Houghton Mifflin
Company, copyright © 1947, p. 78.
4. *Ibid.*, p. 90.
5. *Ibid.*, p. 150.
6. Victoria Case and Robert Ormond Case, *We Called It Culture,*
Brandt & Brandt, copyright © 1948, p. 31.
7. Jesse Lyman Hurlbut, D.D., *The Story Of The Chautauqua,*
G.P. Putnam's Sons, copyright © 1921.
8. Case and Case, p. 131.
9. *Ibid.*, pp. 61-70.
10. Hurlbut, pp. 111-112.

Chapter 8
1. Paxton Hibben, *The Peerless Leader; William Jennings Bryan,*
Russell & Russell, edited and completed by C. Hartley Grattan,
copyright © 1967, pp. 51-52.
2. Charles Morrow Wilson, *The Commoner,* Doubleday &
Company, Inc., copyright © 1970, pp. 119-120.
3. *Ibid.*, p. 294.
4. *Ibid.*, pp. 329-330.
5. *Ibid.*, pp. 128-129.

Chapter 9
1. MacFadden, p. 849.
2. *A Hundred Years From Now,* Edward B. Marks Music Corporation. Copyrighted ©.

3. Macfadden, advertisement from book.
4. *Ibid.*, p. 85.
5. *Ibid.*, pp. 86-87.
6. *Ibid.*, p. 524.
7. *Ibid.*, p. 581.

Chapter 10

1. Marcus Bach, *The Chiropractic Story,* Devorss & Co., copyright © 1968, p. 15.
2. *Ibid.*, p. 22.
3. *Ibid.*, p. 22.
4. *Ibid.*, pp. 137-138.
5. Chester Wilk, *Chiropractic Speaks Out,* Wilk Publishing Co., copyright © 1973, p. 30.
6. Bach, p. 102.
7. *Ibid.*, p. 102.

Chapter 11

1. Elbert Hubbard, *Roycroft Dictionary,* Wm. H. Wise and Co., copyright © 1914.
2. Darrow, pp. 8-14.
3. *Ibid.*, pp. 22-23.
4. *Ibid.*, p. 23.
5. *Ibid.*, p. 24.
6. *Ibid.*, p. 25.
7. *Ibid.*, p. 29.
8. *Ibid.*, p. 92.
9. *Ibid.*, p. 277.
10. *Ibid.*, p. 53.

Chapter 17

1. Frank Lewis Dyer and Thomas Commerford Martin, with William Henry Meadowcroft, *Edison: His Life and Inventions,* Vol. II, copyright © 1929, p. 758.
2. *Ibid.*, pp. 758-759.
3. Roger Burlingame, *Henry Ford,* Alfred A. Knopf, copyright © 1954, p. 7.
4. *Ibid.*, pp. 95-96.
5. *Ibid.*, pp. 103-104.
6. *Ibid.*, p. 27.

Chapter 22

1. Helen Andrews Guthrie, *Introductory Nutrition,* ed. 3, C.V. Mosby Co., copyright © 1975.